The Wiersbe

BIBLE STUDY SERIES

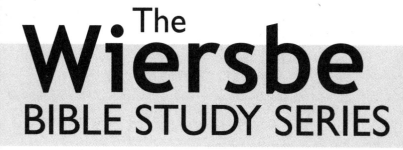

The
Wiersbe
BIBLE STUDY SERIES

PROVERBS

God's

Guidebook to

Wise Living

DAVID C COOK

transforming lives together

THE WIERSBE BIBLE STUDY SERIES: PROVERBS
Published by David C Cook
4050 Lee Vance Drive
Colorado Springs, CO 80918 U.S.A.

Integrity Music Limited, a Division of David Cook
Brighton, East Sussex BN1 2RE, England

DAVID C COOK® and related marks are registered trademarks of David C Cook.

All Scripture quotations in this study are taken from the *New International
Version of the Bible*. *NIV*. Copyright © 1973, 1978, 1984 by International
Bible Society. Used by permission of Zondervan. All rights reserved.

In the *Be Skillful* excerpts, all Scripture quotations, unless otherwise noted, are
taken from the King James Version of the Bible. (Public Domain.) Scripture
quotations marked NKJV are taken from the New King James Version. Copyright
© 1982 by Thomas Nelson, Inc. Used by permission. All rights reserved;
and NASB are taken from the *New American Standard Bible*, © Copyright
1960, 1995 by The Lockman Foundation. Used by permission.

All excerpts taken from *Be Skillful,* second edition, published by David C Cook
in 2009 © 1995 Warren W. Wiersbe, ISBN 978-1-4347-6733-2

ISBN 978-1-4347-6511-6
eISBN 978-0-7814-0378-8

© 2010 Warren W. Wiersbe

The Team: Steve Parolini, Karen Lee-Thorp, Amy Kiechlin,
Sarah Schultz, Jack Campbell, and Karen Athen
Series Cover Design: John Hamilton Design
Cover Photo: Veer Inc.

Printed in the United States of America
First Edition 2010

17 18 19 20 21 22 23 24 25 26

101623

Contents

Introduction to Proverbs

One Word: Wisdom

What is the major theme of the book of Proverbs? One word answers the question: *wisdom*. In Proverbs, the words *wise* and *wisdom* are used at least 125 times, because the aim of the book is to help us acquire and apply God's wisdom to the decisions and activities of daily life.

The book of Proverbs belongs to what scholars call the Wisdom Literature of the Old Testament, which also includes Job and Ecclesiastes. The writers of these books wrestled with some of the most difficult questions of life as they sought to understand life's problems from God's point of view.

Wisdom was an important commodity in the ancient Near East; every ruler had his council of "wise men" whom he consulted when making important decisions. We also need wisdom in order to smartly use our knowledge as well as to listen to others and, of course, to God.

What Wisdom Does

Biblical wisdom begins with a right relationship with the Lord. The wise person believes that there is a God, that He is the Creator and Ruler of all things, and that He has put within His creation a divine order that, if obeyed, leads ultimately to success.

In the Old Testament, the Hebrew word for wise (*hakam*) is used to describe people skillful in working with their hands, such as the artisans who helped build the tabernacle. Wisdom isn't something theoretical; it's something very practical that affects every area of life. It gives order and purpose to life, it gives discernment in making decisions, and it provides a sense of fulfillment in life to the glory of God. Wisdom keeps us in harmony with the principles and purposes that the Lord has built into His world so that as we obey God, everything works for us and not against us.

The Author

In Proverbs 1:1; 10:1; and 25:1, we're told that King Solomon is the author of the proverbs in this book. God gave Solomon great wisdom (1 Kings 3:5–15) so that people came from the ends of the earth to listen to him and returned home amazed (1 Kings 4:29–34; Matt. 12:42). He spoke three thousand proverbs, most of which are not included in this book. The Holy Spirit selected only those proverbs that the people of God should understand and obey in every age.

A Note about How This Study Is Arranged

The first nine chapters of Proverbs form a unit in which the emphasis is on "wisdom" and "folly," personified as two women. Chapters 10—15 form the next unit and present a series of contrasts between the life of wisdom and the life of folly. The closing chapters of the book (16—31) contain a variety of proverbs that gives us counsel about many important areas of life.

In the first three lessons of this study, we'll look at specific sections of Proverbs from the first nine chapters of the book—largely treating the passages in order. However, in the seven lessons that follow, we'll examine a variety of passages in Proverbs arranged by topic.

It will be helpful for you to read through the entire book of Proverbs before beginning this study.

—*Warren W. Wiersbe*

How to Use This Study

This study is designed for both individual and small-group use. We've divided it into eleven lessons—each references one or more chapters in Warren W. Wiersbe's commentary *Be Skillful* (second edition, David C. Cook, 2009). While reading *Be Skillful* is not a prerequisite for going through this study, the additional insights and background Wiersbe offers can greatly enhance your study experience.

The **Getting Started** questions at the beginning of each lesson offer you an opportunity to record your first thoughts and reactions to the study text. This is an important step in the study process as those "first impressions" often include clues about what it is your heart is longing to discover.

The bulk of the study is found in the **Going Deeper** questions. These dive into the Bible text and, along with helpful excerpts from Wiersbe's commentary, help you examine not only the original context and meaning of the verses but also modern application.

Looking Inward narrows the focus down to your personal story. These intimate questions can be a bit uncomfortable at times, but don't shy away from honesty here. This is where you are asked to stand before the mirror of God's Word and look closely at what you see. It's the place to take a good look at yourself in light of the lesson and search for ways in which you can grow in faith.

Going Forward is the place where you can commit to paper those things you want or need to do in order to better live out the discoveries you made in the Looking Inward section. Don't skip or skim through this. Take the time to really consider what practical steps you might take to move closer to Christ. Then share your thoughts with a trusted friend who can act as an encourager and accountability partner.

Finally, there is a brief **Seeking Help** section to close the lesson. This is a reminder for you to invite God into your spiritual-growth process. If you choose to write out a prayer in this section, come back to it as you work through the lesson and continue to seek the Holy Spirit's guidance as you discover God's will for your life.

Tips for Small Groups

A small group is a dynamic thing. One week it might seem like a group of close-knit friends. The next it might seem more like a group of uncomfortable strangers. A small-group leader's role is to read these subtle changes and adjust the tone of the discussion accordingly.

Small groups need to be safe places for people to talk openly. It is through shared wrestling with difficult life issues that some of the greatest personal growth is discovered. But in order for the group to feel safe, participants need to know it's okay *not* to share sometimes. Always invite honest disclosure, but never force someone to speak if he or she isn't comfortable doing so. (A savvy leader will follow up later with a group member who isn't comfortable sharing in a group setting to see if a one-on-one discussion is more appropriate.)

Have volunteers take turns reading excerpts from Scripture or from the commentary. The more each person is involved even in the mundane tasks, the more they'll feel comfortable opening up in more meaningful ways.

The leader should watch the clock and keep the discussion moving. Sometimes there may be more Going Deeper questions than your group can cover in your available time. If you've had a fruitful discussion, it's okay to move on without finishing everything. And if you think the group is getting bogged down on a question or has taken off on a tangent, you can simply say, "Let's go on to question 5." Be sure to save at least ten to fifteen minutes for the Going Forward questions.

Finally, soak your group meetings in prayer—before you begin, during as needed, and always at the end of your time together.

Listen Carefully
(PROVERBS 1:7–33; 8—9)

Before you begin …
- *Pray for the Holy Spirit to reveal truth and wisdom as you go through this lesson.*
- *Read Proverbs 1:7–33; 8—9. This lesson references chapter 2 in* Be Skillful. *It will be helpful for you to have your Bible and a copy of the commentary available as you work through this lesson.*

Getting Started

From the Commentary

> There are times when about the only way you can protect your sanity and your hearing is to open your mouth and say something, even if it's only a primal scream.

> But the greatest tragedy of life isn't that people invade our privacy, get on our nerves, and help destroy our delicate hearing apparatus. The greatest tragedy is that there's so much noise that *people can't hear the things they really need*

to hear. God is trying to get through to them with the voice of wisdom, but all they hear are the confused communications clutter, foolish voices that lead them further away from the truth. Even without our modern electronic noisemakers, a similar situation existed in ancient Israel when Solomon wrote Proverbs, because there's really nothing new under the sun. God was speaking to people in Solomon's day, but they weren't listening.

—*Be Skillful,* pages 31–32

1. What was the "noise" that kept the ancient Israelites from hearing God's truth? Based on your impression of Proverbs so far, how significant a problem was this in Solomon's time? How much of a problem is it today? What are some of the things that keep us from hearing God today?

Simplicity
folly
the "world"
   "you do you"
   "independent" women
   "your truth"

2. Choose one verse or phrase from Proverbs 1:7–33; 8—9 that stands out to you. This could be something you're intrigued by, something that makes you uncomfortable, something that puzzles you, something that resonates with you, or just something you want to examine further. Write that here.

"The fear of the LORD is hatred of evil." 9:13
"If you are wise, you are wise for yourself;
if you scoff, you alone will bear it." 9:12

Going Deeper

From the Commentary

> [Proverbs 1:8–10, 15–19 refers to the] voice of a godly
> father urging his son to listen to Wisdom and obey what
> he hears. Note that both the father and the mother have
> been involved in teaching the boy, and they both warn
> him not to abandon what he's been told.
>
> —*Be Skillful*, page 32

3. Read Deuteronomy 6:6–9. In what ways have the parents described in
Proverbs 1:8–10, 15–19 obeyed these instructions? What is the point of all
this teaching? What is the parents' desire?

For their child to obey – loving
God & others. They are teaching
wisdom and avoiding unwise

*More to Consider: Read Titus 2:10. How can parents "adorn
the doctrine" of God or "make the teaching about God our Savior
attractive"? How can this help in the raising of godly children?*

From the Commentary

> Anybody who makes it easy for us to disobey God certainly isn't a friend. The offer they made sounded exciting, but it only led to disaster. How tragic that a group of people would actually find enjoyment in doing evil, and how foolish of them to think their loot would satisfy their desires. They rejected the eternal treasures of wisdom (3:14–16; 16:16) for the cheap trinkets of this world, and they lost their souls in the bargain.
>
> —*Be Skillful*, page 33

4. Read Proverbs 1:10–14. Who is this passage referring to? What makes following evil so compelling? What are the promises of evil? How do they compare with the promises of God?

From Today's World

If you were to flip through television channels any evening during any given week, you'd likely come across at least one "reality" TV show. While the formats of these shows vary greatly, the concept is essentially the same: Put a bunch of people in a somewhat controlled setting and then see what happens when they're confronted with problems or challenges. However, a close examination of many of these shows will reveal that the "reality" behind the genre is more controlled and manipulated than the title might suggest. In some shows, people are even pitted against each other by the design of the producers or the function of the challenges in order to create a more "compelling" TV show. Not surprisingly, it is the shows that illustrate the baser nature of humankind (backstabbing, secret dealings, lying, cheating, etc.) that get the most press.

5. What is it about "reality" television that draws so many viewers? What does this say about the draw of darkness? How are we, as Christians, supposed to respond to these sorts of things? What might Solomon say to those who are intrigued by them?

From the Commentary

To whom does Wisdom speak? To three classes of sinners: the simple ones, the scorners (scoffers, mockers, NIV), and the fools (Prov. 1:22). The *simple* are naive people who believe anything (14:15) but examine nothing. They're gullible and easily led astray. *Scorners* think they know everything (21:24) and laugh at the things that are really important. While the simple one has a blank look on his face, the scorner wears a sneer. *Fools* are people who are ignorant of truth because they're dull and stubborn. Their problem isn't a low IQ or poor education; their problem is a lack of spiritual desire to seek and find God's wisdom.

—*Be Skillful*, page 34

6. In today's terms, how would you define the three classes of sinners that Wisdom speaks to (the simple, the scorners, and the fools)? Why does each of these groups of people need wisdom? How does (or can) the church deal with each of these groups?

From the Commentary

Wisdom's words are plain, spoken clearly and openly so that there can be no confusion. Of course, those who reject the Lord don't understand what God is saying (1 Cor. 2:12–16), but this isn't because the Word of God is confusing or unclear. It's because sinners are spiritually blind and deaf (Matt. 13:14–15). The problem is with the hearer, not the speaker.

—*Be Skillful*, page 36

7. What are some of the clear messages found in Proverbs 1:7–33; 8—9? How might those who are not looking for truth miss these messages? What are some examples of this in your experience?

From the Commentary

Wisdom has better gifts to offer than perishable riches—blessings like prudence, knowledge, discretion ("witty inventions," Prov. 8:12), the fear of the Lord, humility, godly speech, wise counsel, understanding, guidance on life's path, strength for the journey, and "durable riches." A life that's enriched by God may be poor in this world's goods, but it is rich in the things that matter most. It's good to enjoy the things that money can buy, provided you don't lose the things that money can't buy. *What wisdom has to offer can't be purchased anywhere, no matter how rich you are.*

—*Be Skillful*, page 37

8. Why are the gifts that Wisdom offers better than material riches? Why are material riches often perceived as more valuable? How can the gifts Wisdom offers make a lasting difference in the life of the recipient? In the lives of those around him or her?

From the Commentary

> In Proverbs 8, we saw Wisdom at work in creation, but in Proverbs 9 we see her having built a spacious house ("seven pillars"), where she prepares a sumptuous banquet. The Jewish people didn't use their flocks and herds for food, so opportunities to eat roast beef or lamb were infrequent and welcomed. The table would be spread with delectable foods as well as wine to drink.
>
> Note that [Wisdom's maidens (Prov. 9:3–9)] are inviting one class of people: the simple (Prov. 9:4). Wisdom's first call was to the simple, the scorners, and the fools (1:22). The scorners laughed at her, so in her second call she invited only the simple and the fools (8:5). But the fools didn't want God's wisdom, so in this third call she invites only the simple ones to come to her feast.
>
> —*Be Skillful*, pages 38–39

9. What does this diminishing invitation list as noted in Proverbs 9:3–9 say about God's invitation to us? What does it look like to respond to Wisdom's invitation?

From the Commentary

> When you respond to Wisdom's invitation and attend the feast, what will you receive? For one thing, you'll have a greater respect for the Lord and a deeper knowledge of the Holy One (Prov. 9:10). The better you know God, the keener will be your knowledge and discernment when it comes to the decisions of life.
>
> —*Be Skillful*, page 40

10. What does Wisdom promise in 9:11? What is the message of 9:12? What is the woman Folly's invitation (9:13–18)? What is the proper response to her call?

Looking Inward

Take a moment to reflect on all that you've explored thus far in this study of Proverbs 1:7–33; 8—9. Review your notes and answers and think about how each of these things matters in your life today.

Tips for Small Groups: To get the most out of this section, form pairs or trios and have group members take turns answering these questions. Be honest and as open as you can in this discussion, but most of all, be encouraging and supportive of others. Be sensitive to those who are going through particularly difficult times and don't press for people to speak if they're uncomfortable doing so.

11. What are examples of the "noise" that keeps you from listening to God? How can you go about turning down the noise? What are some of the lessons Wisdom is trying to teach you that you have a hard time hearing?

12. Have you ever been simple, a scorner, or a fool? Describe that experience. How might wisdom have helped you in those circumstances? In what ways do you still find yourself in one or more of these groups of sinners?

13. How has wisdom helped you grow closer to God? What are some practical applications of the wisdom you have embraced?

Going Forward

14. Think of one or two things that you have learned that you'd like to work on in the coming week. Remember that this is all about quality, not quantity. It's better to work on one specific area of life and do it well than to work on many and do poorly (or to be so overwhelmed that you simply don't try).

Do you need to stop being a "scorner" in one or more areas of your life? Do you need to turn down the noise that keeps you from hearing God? Be specific. Go back through Proverbs 1:7–33; 8—9 and put a star next to the phrase or verse that is most encouraging to you. Consider memorizing this verse.

Real-Life Application Ideas: Do a self-evaluation of the "noises" that surround your life. List all the things that fill your day and take your attention. Are all of these things necessary to your life? Consider how you might go about creating more space to listen to Wisdom.

Seeking Help

15. Write a prayer below (or simply pray one in silence), inviting God to work on your mind and heart in those areas you've previously noted. Be honest about your desires and fears.

Notes for Small Groups:

- *Look for ways to put into practice the things you wrote in the Going Forward section. Talk with other group members about your ideas and commit to being accountable to one another.*

- *During the coming week, ask the Holy Spirit to continue to reveal truth to you from what you've read and studied.*

- *Before you start the next lesson, read Proverbs 2—4. For more in-depth lesson preparation, read chapter 3, "The Path of Wisdom and Life," in* Be Skillful.

Wisdom and Life
(PROVERBS 2—4)

Before you begin ...
- *Pray for the Holy Spirit to reveal truth and wisdom as you go through this lesson.*
- *Read Proverbs 2—4. This lesson references chapter 3 in* Be Skillful. *It will be helpful for you to have your Bible and a copy of the commentary available as you work through this lesson.*

Getting Started

From the Commentary

In the book of Proverbs, the words *path* and *way* (and their plurals) are found nearly one hundred times (KJV). Wisdom is not only a person to love, but Wisdom is also a path to walk, and the emphasis in [Proverbs] 2, 3, and 4 is on the blessings God's people enjoy when they walk on Wisdom's path. The path of Wisdom leads to life, but the way of Folly leads to death; when you walk on the path of Wisdom, you enjoy three wonderful assurances: Wisdom *protects* your path (ch. 2), *directs* your path (ch. 3), and *perfects* your path (ch. 4).

—*Be Skillful*, pages 44–45

1. Go through Proverbs 2—4 and underline all the references to "path" or "way." What do these verses tell us about the purpose of Proverbs for Christians seeking to know God? How can these verses help direct Christians to their specific path?

2. Choose one verse or phrase from Proverbs 2—4 that stands out to you. This could be something you're intrigued by, something that makes you uncomfortable, something that puzzles you, something that resonates with you, or just something you want to examine further. Write that here.

3: 11-12

Going Deeper

From the Commentary

> The key verse in chapter 2 is verse 8: "He guards the paths of justice, and preserves the way of His saints" (NKJV). The repetition of the phrase "my son" (2:1; 3:1, 11, 21; 4:10, 20; and see 4:1, "my children") reminds us that the book of Proverbs records a loving father's wise counsel to his family. The British statesman Lord Chesterfield said, "In matters of religion and matrimony I never give any advice; because I will not have anybody's torments in this world or the next laid to my charge." But Jewish fathers were *commanded* to teach their children wisdom (Deut. 6:1–9); if the children were smart, they paid attention and obeyed.
>
> —*Be Skillful*, page 44

3. Why do you think the author of Proverbs uses the analogy of a father sharing wisdom with his son to pass along the lessons? How might this be perceived today, in a culture where parents don't always have a good relationship with their children? In what ways is this depiction like other portions of Scripture where God is referred to as "Father"?

More to Consider: Read Proverbs 2:4; 3:13–15; 8:10–21; 16:16. According to these verses, what is the "paycheck" that studying wisdom can offer?

From the Commentary

[In Proverbs 2:10–19,] we meet "the evil man" and "the strange woman," two people who are dangerous because they want to lead God's children away from the path of life. The evil man is known for his perverse ("froward," KJV; crooked) words (see vv. 12, 14; 6:14; 8:13; 10:31–32; 16:28, 30). He walks on the dark path of disobedience and enjoys doing that which is evil. He belongs to the crowd Solomon warns us about in 1:10–19. The person who walks in the way of wisdom would immediately detect his deceit and avoid him.

—*Be Skillful*, pages 45–46

4. Who are the "evil man" and "strange woman" referred to in Proverbs 2:10–19? In what ways do we run into such people in modern culture? How can we recognize them? What are we to do when we encounter them? How does wisdom help us make good choices when confronting these people?

From the History Books

Between the fifteenth and eighteenth centuries AD, witch hunts became a hallmark of the church's attempt to identify and eliminate people deemed dangerous because of their association with satanic or pagan rituals and involvement with the supernatural. Many accused witches were burned at the stake for their purported crimes against the church. While this occurred primarily in Europe (especially Germany), the witch hunting continued onto the shores of America, perhaps most famously with the Salem witch trials in 1692–1693.

5. What "wisdom" might have prompted the actions that led to witch hunts? How was that core idea a good thing? How was its enactment a bad thing? In what ways do people today still conduct witch hunts? What is the difference between identifying evil people in order to avoid them and identifying them in order to eliminate them? Is it our job to eradicate evil? Why or why not?

From the Commentary

If we receive God's words and obey them, *then* we will have wisdom to make wise decisions, and *thus* God will keep His promise and protect us from the evil man and the strange woman. When you obey God, you have the privilege to "walk in the ways of good men" (v. 20 NIV). *If you follow the Word of God, you will never lack for the right kind of friends.*

—*Be Skillful*, page 46

6. What does it mean to "walk in the ways of good men" (Prov. 2:20)? How do you know whether you are walking in these ways?

From the Commentary

The key verses in [Proverbs 3] are verses 5–6, a promise God's people have often claimed as they have sought the Lord's direction for their lives. And this promise has never failed them—if they have obeyed the conditions God has laid down in verses 1–12.

—*Be Skillful*, page 47

7. What are the conditions God lays down in Proverbs 3:1–12? What promises does God offer to those who follow these conditions? How do we go about following these conditions in today's society?

From the Commentary

> If we trust and obey, our Father will direct our path into the blessings He has planned for us; the first of these blessings is the *true wealth that comes from wisdom* (vv. 13–18).
>
> Another blessing is *harmony with God's creation* (Prov. 3:19–20).
>
> A third blessing is *the Father's providential care* (3:21–26).
>
> *A positive relationship with others* (3:27–35) is a fourth blessing.
>
> —*Be Skillful*, pages 48–50

8. What is the wealth that comes with wisdom (Prov. 3:13–18)? What does "harmony with God's creation" mean (3:19–20)? What is God's providential care (3:21–26)? What does the blessing of a positive relationship look like (3:27–35)?

From the Commentary

> The key verse in chapter 4 is verse 18: "But the path of the just is as the shining light, that shineth more and more unto the perfect day." The picture is that of the sunrise ("the first gleam of dawn," NIV) and the increasing of the light on the pilgrim path as the day advances. If we walk in the way of God's wisdom, the path gets brighter and brighter and there is no sunset! When the path ends, we step into a land where the light never dims, for "there shall be no night there" (Rev. 22:5).
>
> —*Be Skillful*, pages 50–51

9. What does the "path of the just" look like in the modern church? How does today's church seek wisdom? What are some ways the church can do a better job of walking in the path of the just? What are some examples from your experience that illustrate how the path of the just "shines"?

More to Consider: Proverbs 4:5–7 suggests that we should "buy" wisdom. What is the implied "cost" of wisdom? How do we pay that cost?

From the Commentary

> If you are willing to do God's will, you will have God's guidance (John 7:17), but if you treat God's will like a buffet lunch, choosing only what pleases you, He will never direct you.… The will of God isn't for the curious; it's for the serious. As we look back on more than forty years of marriage and ministry, my wife and I can testify to God's providential leading in our lives in ways that we never suspected He would use.
>
> But God's children can't expect God's leading if they shuttle back and forth between the path of wisdom and the path of the wicked (Prov. 4:14–17). Stay as far away from that path as you can!
>
> *—Be Skillful*, page 52

10. In what ways do people "shuttle back and forth" between the path of wisdom and the path of the wicked? How common is this? Why is it difficult to stay on the path of the wise? What are some ways that we can avoid giving in to the temptation offered by the path of the wicked?

Looking Inward

Take a moment to reflect on all that you've explored thus far in this study of Proverbs 2—4. Review your notes and answers and think about how each of these things matters in your life today.

Tips for Small Groups: To get the most out of this section, form pairs or trios and have group members take turns answering these questions. Be honest and as open as you can in this discussion, but most of all, be encouraging and supportive of others. Be sensitive to those who are going through particularly difficult times and don't press for people to speak if they're uncomfortable doing so.

11. What are specific examples that show whether or not you are following the path of the wise? How has the wisdom of Proverbs helped you in following that path? What is the "paycheck" you have received from studying wisdom?

12. Who are the "evil man" and "strange woman" in your daily experience? What makes their ways appealing to you? When have you chosen to follow them instead of wisdom? What are some ways to avoid doing that in the future?

13. How well are you following the conditions provided in Proverbs 3:1–12? What are some things you can do to better follow these conditions? What impact would that have on your faith life? Your relationship with others?

Going Forward

14. Think of one or two things that you have learned that you'd like to work on in the coming week. Remember that this is all about quality, not quantity. It's better to work on one specific area of life and do it well than to work on many and do poorly (or to be so overwhelmed that you simply don't try).

Do you need to study the path of the wise? Do you need to avoid being drawn to evil? Be specific. Go back through Proverbs 2—4 and put a star next to the phrase or verse that is most encouraging to you. Consider memorizing this verse.

Real-Life Application Ideas: Draw a timeline of your life from birth until today. Along that line, make marks to indicate good seasons of life and seasons when you were following a darker path. Now draw that line out into the future. Think of some practical ways that can help you to continue marking "wise decisions" along the line. (These might include spending more time in prayer, involving yourself more with people who are a positive influence, and so on.) Then make a commitment to doing these things, remembering that God's grace is sufficient for those times when you stray from the good path.

Seeking Help

15. Write a prayer below (or simply pray one in silence), inviting God to work on your mind and heart in those areas you've previously noted. Be honest about your desires and fears.

Notes for Small Groups:

- *Look for ways to put into practice the things you wrote in the Going Forward section. Talk with other group members about your ideas and commit to being accountable to one another.*

- *During the coming week, ask the Holy Spirit to continue to reveal truth to you from what you've read and studied.*

- *Before you start the next lesson, read Proverbs 5—7. For more in-depth lesson preparation, read chapter 4, "The Path of Folly and Death," in* Be Skillful.

9/8

-praying for areas where you need more wisdom

-God sees & knows the whole picture

Folly and Death
(PROVERBS 5—7)

Before you begin …
- *Pray for the Holy Spirit to reveal truth and wisdom as you go through this lesson.*
- *Read Proverbs 5—7. This lesson references chapter 4 in* Be Skillful. *It will be helpful for you to have your Bible and a copy of the commentary available as you work through this lesson.*

Getting Started

From the Commentary

"You shall not commit adultery."

The Lord God spoke those words at Mount Sinai, and we call what He said the seventh commandment (Ex. 20:14). It declares that sexual intimacy outside the bonds of marriage is wrong, even if "between consenting adults." This law specifically mentions adultery, but the commandment includes the sexual sins prohibited elsewhere in Scripture

(Lev. 18; Rom. 1:18–32; 1 Cor. 6:9–20; Eph. 5:1–14). God invented sex and has every right to tell us how to use it properly.

However, on hearing the seventh commandment, many people in contemporary society smile nonchalantly and ask, "What's wrong with premarital or extramarital sex, or any other kind, for that matter?" After all, they argue, many people indulge in these things and seem to get away with it.

Why worry about sexual sins? These three chapters of Proverbs give us three reasons why we should worry if we break God's laws of purity: because sexual sin is eventually disappointing (Prov. 5), gradually destructive (ch. 6), and ultimately deadly (ch. 7). That's why God says "You shall not commit adultery."

—*Be Skillful,* pages 59–60

1. Why do you think Solomon focuses on the topic of purity in Proverbs 5—7? What are the physical and emotional consequences of adultery and sexual sin? Beyond even the moral implications, what spiritual lessons can we discover from this teaching?

unplanned pregnancies, STDs
emotional ties not easily broken

leads to death!
even though it "sounds" harmless
and loving.

2. Choose one verse or phrase from Proverbs 5—7 that stands out to you. This could be something you're intrigued by, something that makes you uncomfortable, something that puzzles you, something that resonates with you, or just something you want to examine further. Write that here.

" All at once he follows her, as an ox goes to the slaughter... " Prov. 7:22

Going Deeper

From the Commentary

When married people honor and respect sex as God instructs them in His Word, they can experience increasing enjoyment and enrichment in their intimacy. But when people break the rules, the result is just the opposite. They experience disappointment and disillusionment and have to search for larger "doses" of sexual adventure in order to attain the imaginary pleasure level they're seeking.

God created sex not only for reproduction, but also for enjoyment, and He didn't put the "marriage wall" around sex to *rob us* of pleasure but to *increase* pleasure and *protect* it. In chapter 5, Solomon explains the disappointments that come when people violate God's loving laws of sexual purity.

—*Be Skillful*, page 60

3. What is the "marriage wall" referenced above? How does this wall help married couples avoid the disappointments Solomon describes in Proverbs 5? Why are people still drawn to sexual sin even if they know they'll ultimately experience disappointment or disillusionment?

only allowing things in the confines
of marriage; protection around the
covenant.

it's worldly and people don't fully
understand the implications.
protecting marriage from sexual
immorality

More to Consider: *The word translated "strange" in reference to "the strange woman" basically means "not related to." What is the allure of the strange woman? (See Prov. 7:13–20.) What is the ultimate outcome of an alliance with someone who is not your spouse (5:4)? Why is that the case?*

2 edged sword
            death

From the Commentary

The book of Proverbs emphasizes the importance of *looking ahead* to see where your actions will lead you. The wise person checks on the destination before buying a ticket (4:26), but modern society thinks that people can violate God's laws and escape the consequences. They're sure that whatever has happened to others will never happen to them. Sad to say, their ignorance and insolence can never neutralize the tragic aftermath that comes when people break the laws of God.

—*Be Skillful*, page 61

4. Read the following verses: Proverbs 5:11; 14:12–14; 16:25; 19:20; 20:21; 23:17–18, 32; 24:14, 20; 25:8. What does each of these passages say about considering the consequences of your actions? How do they apply to Proverbs 5's emphasis on sexual purity? What are some of the consequences of breaking God's law regarding purity?

From the History Books

The 1960s are often associated with the "sexual revolution" in American culture. The release of the Kinsey Reports a few years earlier, the invention of the birth-control pill, and the rise of the women's liberation movement probably were three of the greatest factors contributing to this sudden change in cultural morality. During this season of change, sexuality was taken "out of the closet" and turned into a subject worthy of public dialogue. One of the most famous slogans from that time period, "Make love, not war," not only expresses an opinion on the Vietnam War, it invites the topic of sexuality into the public consciousness.

5. Why do you think history refers to the 1960s as a time of "sexual revolution"? What does this say about the way sex was perceived (and acknowledged) in the decades that preceded the 1960s? What does it say about the importance and compelling nature of sexuality? How might this era in our culture be similar to what Solomon was referring to in Proverbs 5—7? What makes sexuality such a controversial subject in society today (especially in the church)?

From the Commentary

> Freedom of choice is one of the privileges God has given us, but He instructs us and urges us to use that freedom wisely. The laws of God are guideposts to lead us on the path of life, and He watches the decisions we make and the roads we take. "The eyes of the LORD are in every place, beholding the evil and the good" (15:3).
>
> —*Be Skillful*, page 63

6. How do people abuse "freedom of choice" when it comes to their sexuality? How does the abuse of this freedom of choice actually result in the loss of freedom? What does true freedom in Christ look like?

From the Commentary

> Chapter 6 deals with three enemies that can destroy a person financially, physically, morally, or spiritually: unwise financial commitments (vv. 1–5), laziness (vv. 6–11), and lust (vv. 20–35). It is not unusual for one person to be guilty of all three, because laziness and lust often go together; people who can easily be pressured into putting up security for somebody can be pressured into doing other foolish things, including committing adultery. "For where your treasure is, there will your heart be also" (Matt. 6:21).
>
> —*Be Skillful*, page 64

7. How are the three enemies that can destroy a person as described in Proverbs 6 similar? How are they different? Why does Solomon speak so

strongly about each of these enemies? Why is their power so destructive? What can we do to avoid that destruction?

From the Commentary

Hunger is a strong force in human life, and the only way to satisfy hunger is to eat, but if you steal the bread that you eat, you're breaking the law. You'll end up paying more for that bread than if you'd gone out and bought a loaf at the bakery.

Adultery is stealing.

King David was a brilliant strategist on the battlefield and a wise ruler on the throne, but he lost his common sense when he gazed at his neighbor's wife and lusted for her (2 Sam. 12). He was sure he could get away with his sin, but common sense would have told him he was wrong. Every stratagem David used to implicate Bathsheba's husband failed, so he ended up having the man killed. Surely David knew that we reap what we sow, and reap he did, right in the harvest field of his own family.

—*Be Skillful*, page 66

8. Why is adultery a form of theft? In what ways do people lose their good sense (Prov. 6:32) when committing sexual sins such as adultery? What are some arguments a person might make to defend his or her adultery? What is the flaw in each argument?

More to Consider: In today's culture the impact of a sexual scandal is often multiplied by the power of the media. In what ways does today's society prove the truth noted in Proverbs 6:33–35?

From the Commentary

[In Proverbs 7,] for the third time Solomon calls the young person back to the Word of God (vv. 1–5), because keeping God's commandments is a matter of life or death. The adulteress lives on a dead-end street: "Her house is the way to hell, going down to the chambers of death" (v. 27).

The familiar phrase "apple of your eye" (v. 2 NKJV) refers to the pupil of the eye, which the ancients thought was a sphere like an apple. We protect our eyes because they're valuable to us, and so should we honor and protect God's

Word by obeying it. Sexual sin often begins with undisciplined eyes and hands (Matt. 5:27–30), but the heart of the problem is ... the heart (Prov. 7:2–3).

—*Be Skillful*, page 67

9. Why do you think Solomon uses such dramatic language in Proverbs 7 to describe the consequences of following the adulteress? In what ways is this wisdom true today? What sort of "death" comes from committing sexual sin?

From the Commentary

When we pray, "Lead us not into temptation" (Matt. 6:13), we know that God doesn't tempt us (James 1:13–16); yet we may tempt ourselves, tempt others, and even tempt God (Ex. 17:1–7; Num. 14:22; Deut. 6:16; Ps. 78:18, 56; 1 Cor. 10:9). We tempt God when we deliberately disobey Him and put ourselves into situations so difficult that only God can deliver us. It's as though we "dare Him" to do something.

—*Be Skillful*, page 69

10. What are some examples of how people tempt God by deliberately getting into morally risky situations? Why is it so easy to fall into this trap? How does a conscious decision to disobey God reflect and affect the manner in which we understand God's grace? Does God still offer grace and forgiveness when we deliberately tempt Him with disobedience? If so, what then should compel His followers to walk a wiser path?

Looking Inward

Take a moment to reflect on all that you've explored thus far in this study of Proverbs 5—7. Review your notes and answers and think about how each of these things matters in your life today.

Tips for Small Groups: To get the most out of this section, form pairs or trios and have group members take turns answering these questions. Be honest and as open as you can in this discussion, but most of all, be encouraging and supportive of others. Be sensitive to those who are going through particularly difficult times and don't press for people to speak if they're uncomfortable doing so.

11. How comfortable are you with the topic of purity? If you've struggled with this issue in your personal life, where have you turned for help? What are the greatest challenges you've faced in this area of your life? (If you're in a small-group setting, you don't need to share your answers aloud. Instead, spend time in thoughtful reflection and prayer, asking God to reveal His wisdom.)

12. If you are married, think of ways you've honored the wisdom Solomon reveals through his examination of sexual sin in Proverbs 5—7. Look only at the positive things for a moment. How do these things prove Solomon's wisdom? What are two or three things you wish those who struggle with sexual sin could learn from Solomon?

13. How have you been tempted to exercise your "freedom of choice" in ways that don't honor God? Why is the freedom God gives you sometimes difficult to understand? What are some of the things you're doing in your life to better understand what it means to have freedom of choice as a follower of God?

Going Forward

14. Think of one or two things that you have learned that you'd like to work on in the coming week. Remember that this is all about quality, not quantity. It's better to work on one specific area of life and do it well than to work on many and do poorly (or to be so overwhelmed that you simply don't try).

Do you need to change some of your thoughts or habits regarding sexuality? Be specific. Go back through Proverbs 5—7 and put a star next to the phrase or verse that is most encouraging to you. Consider memorizing this verse.

Real-Life Application Ideas: If you're married, spend time talking with your spouse about the warnings in Proverbs 5—7. Talk about how you can work together to avoid the temptations of sexual sin. And if you have children, discuss how you'll present these truths to them and at what age.

Seeking Help

15. Write a prayer below (or simply pray one in silence), inviting God to work on your mind and heart in those areas you've previously noted. Be honest about your desires and fears.

Notes for Small Groups:

- *Look for ways to put into practice the things you wrote in the Going Forward section. Talk with other group members about your ideas and commit to being accountable to one another.*

- *During the coming week, ask the Holy Spirit to continue to reveal truth to you from what you've read and studied.*

- *The next lesson references a variety of verses from Proverbs. Come prepared with your Bible to explore the theme "Wise and Otherwise." For more in-depth lesson preparation, read chapters 5–6 in* Be Skillful.

People, Wise and Otherwise

(KEY VERSES: PROVERBS 1:7; 2:1–22; 3:7; 8:13;
14:6, 15–16; 15:5; 21:24; 26:3–12; 29:9)

*using social media
as "comfort" / to numb
the need for physical comfort*

Before you begin ...

- *Pray for the Holy Spirit to reveal truth and wisdom as you go through this lesson.*
- *This lesson references chapters 5–6 in* Be Skillful. *It will be helpful for you to have your Bible and a copy of the commentary available as you work through this lesson.*

Getting Started

From the Commentary

The book of Proverbs is basically about different kinds of people, what they believe and do, and how they interact with one another. People create circumstances that are good and bad, and you and I have to deal with people and circumstances as we go through life. Solomon's aim in writing this book is to help us become skillful in relating to both people and circumstances so that we can make a success out of life to the glory of God.

—*Be Skillful,* page 75

1. People who are Christians and non-Christians often quote proverbs to one another that come straight out of Scripture (whether they know it or not). From what you've read so far in Proverbs, what makes it such a treasure trove of wisdom? How can the wisdom you've discovered so far be applied to marriages? Friendships? Work relationships? Our relationship with God?

More to Consider: Read 2 Timothy 3:15. How is a saving faith the first step toward wisdom?

2. Read this week's key verses (Prov. 1:7; 2:1–22; 3:7; 8:13; 14:6, 15–16; 15:5; 21:24; 26:3–12; 29:9). Which of these verses is most meaningful to you? Explain.

Going Deeper

From the Commentary

> Wise people listen to wise instruction, especially the Word of God.
>
> This means that we must diligently spend time reading and studying the Word of God, appropriating its truths into our hearts, and obeying what God commands (2:1–9). It isn't enough to own a study Bible and read books about the Bible, helpful as they are. It's one thing to know about the Bible and quite something else to hear God speak through His Word and teach us His wisdom so that we become more like Jesus Christ.
>
> —*Be Skillful*, page 76

3. What are the moral benefits of wisdom as noted in Proverbs 2:1–22? How does wisdom help us to know the right path to take in life? How does discretion protect you (v. 11)? How does it protect you from the adulteress (v. 16)?

From the Commentary

> "The fear of the LORD is the beginning of wisdom" (Prov.
> 1:7). "Do not be wise in your own eyes; fear the LORD and
> depart from evil" (Prov. 3:7 NKJV).… Fearing the Lord
> means respecting Him so that we obey His will and seek
> to honor His name. Fearing the Lord is the opposite of
> tempting the Lord by deliberately disobeying Him and
> then daring Him to intervene.
>
> —*Be Skillful,* page 77

4. Read Philippians 2:12 and Psalm 2:11. How do these verses speak to the
idea that the fear of the Lord is the beginning of wisdom? What are some
practical ways we go about "fearing the Lord" in our daily walk? How is
"fearing the Lord" different from being afraid of God?

From the History Books

Sometimes the charisma of a leader is what draws people to follow him or
her. Throughout history, there are many examples of leaders who gain sub-
stantial followings and then lead them down paths that are anything but
wise. The most notorious of these is certainly Adolf Hitler, whose brilliance
as a strategist and influence over a culture were matched only by the evil

path that he led his people down. But there are many other examples that illustrate how difficult it can be sometimes to know if the person you're following is a wise leader. This is true not only with leaders of nations, but also with leaders of companies and even families.

5. What can compel people to follow leaders who are doing unwise things? What are some good guidelines to heed when considering the leaders you follow? How can Solomon's advice assist in the assessment of potential leaders?

From the Commentary

"A wise man fears and departs from evil, but a fool rages and is self-confident" (14:16 NKJV). If we fear the Lord, we will hate evil (8:13; see Ps. 97:10; Rom. 12:9). The self-confident person isn't wise. Joshua was self-confident and lost a battle (Josh. 7); Samson was self-confident and became a prisoner (Judg. 16:20ff.); Peter was self-confident and betrayed the Lord three times (Luke 22:33–34). "Therefore let him who thinks he stands take heed lest he fall" (1 Cor. 10:12 NKJV).

Wise people don't take unnecessary chances and experiment to see how close they can get to the precipice without falling off.

—*Be Skillful*, page 79

6. What is the difference between appropriate confidence and foolish confidence? What are examples of "unnecessary chances" that fools often take? (Think in terms of the workplace, the home, relationships, and even church situations.) How do you know if you're taking a wise risk and not an unnecessary one?

More to Consider: The wicked and their wickedness are mentioned at least one hundred times in Proverbs. Read Proverbs 6:12–19. How does this passage summarize the wicked? What are the characteristics of someone who is wicked?

From the Commentary

The simple are the naive people who believe everything because they don't have convictions about anything. What they think is sophisticated "tolerance" is only spiritual ignorance, because they lack the ability to discriminate between truth and error. "A simple man believes anything, but a prudent man gives thought to his steps" (14:15 NIV). Charles R. Bridges writes, "To *believe every word* of God is faith. To *believe every word* of man is credulity."

—*Be Skillful*, pages 87–88

7. What are some examples from your experience (or observation) that illustrate the truth "A prudent man gives thought to his steps"? Why is it important to test the words of man when considering them? How do we go about testing those words? How can God's Word help us in that effort?

From the Commentary

Scorners think they know everything, and anybody who tries to teach them is only wasting time. "Proud and haughty scorner [scoffer] is his name" (21:24). Scorners can't find wisdom even if they seek for it (14:6), because learning God's truth demands a humble mind and an obedient will. What scorners lack in knowledge they make up for in arrogance.

—*Be Skillful*, page 89

8. Who are examples of "scorners" in popular culture? What makes these people so arrogant? What is the line between appropriate confidence and inappropriate arrogance?

From the Commentary

> In Proverbs, three different Hebrew words are translated "fool": *kesyl*, the dull, stupid fool who is stubborn; *ewiyl*, the corrupt fool who is morally perverted and unreasonable; and *nabal*, the fool who is like a stubborn animal, the brutish fool. In this summary of the characteristics of the fool, we'll combine the verses and not distinguish the three different types. After all, fools are fools, no matter what name we give them!
>
> [The problem with fools] is their hearts…. "There is no fear of God before their eyes" (Rom. 3:18).
>
> A fool's own father can't instruct him (Prov. 15:5), and if you try to debate with him, it will only lead to trouble (29:9). Why? Because fools actually enjoy their folly and think they're really living!
>
> —*Be Skillful*, page 91

9. What are some modern examples of Solomon's "fools" as described in Proverbs 15:5 and 29:9? Why is it useless to debate with fools? What is the difference between a fool as described in Proverbs and someone who just makes a foolish decision?

From the Commentary

Fools don't learn from their mistakes but go right back to the same old mess, like a dog returning to eat his vomit (Prov. 26:11). Experience is a good teacher for the wise, but not for fools. This verse is quoted in 2 Peter 2:22 as a description of counterfeit believers who follow false teachers. Like a sow that's been washed, they look better on the outside; and like a dog that's vomited, they feel better on the inside; but they're still not sheep! They don't have the divine new nature; consequently, they go right back to the old life. Obedience and perseverance in the things of the Lord are proof of conversion.

—*Be Skillful*, page 96

10. What does Proverbs 26:3–12 teach us about the consequences of giving a fool a job to do? What should our response be to those who choose a life of foolishness?

Looking Inward

Take a moment to reflect on all that you've explored thus far in this study of "People, Wise and Otherwise." Review your notes and answers and think about how each of these things matters in your life today.

Tips for Small Groups: To get the most out of this section, form pairs or trios and have group members take turns answering these questions. Be honest and as open as you can in this discussion, but most of all, be encouraging and supportive of others. Be sensitive to those who are going through particularly difficult times and don't press for people to speak if they're uncomfortable doing so.

11. What are some of the ways you listen to wise instruction? How do you discern between wise and foolish advice?

12. Have you ever followed a leader who was doing unwise things? How did you learn the leader wasn't wise? What did you do in response to this discovery? How does Solomon's advice to avoid following the foolish or evil leader interact with the Scripture passages that teach us to respect authorities, such as Romans 13:1–7?

13. When have you been a scoffer or scorner? What prompted that behavior? What are practical ways to avoid falling into that trap when you're tempted to become arrogant?

Going Forward

14. Think of one or two things that you have learned that you'd like to work on in the coming week. Remember that this is all about quality, not

quantity. It's better to work on one specific area of life and do it well than to work on many and do poorly (or to be so overwhelmed that you simply don't try).

Do you need to put more energy into recognizing and avoiding foolishness? Do you need to work on avoiding arrogance? Be specific. Go back through the key verses in this lesson and put a star next to the phrase or verse that is most encouraging to you. Consider memorizing this verse.

Real-Life Application Ideas: Take an informal survey of friends, coworkers, and family members. Ask them to share any "proverbs" they have about life. Don't prompt them to share specifically from Scripture, just ask for the first thing that comes to mind. Then compare what you collect with what is in Proverbs (an online Bible or concordance program will speed up the process). What does this tell you about the prevalence of Solomon's wisdom? About the ways people interpret wisdom?

Seeking Help

15. Write a prayer below (or simply pray one in silence), inviting God to work on your mind and heart in those areas you've previously noted. Be honest about your desires and fears.

Notes for Small Groups:

- *Look for ways to put into practice the things you wrote in the Going Forward section. Talk with other group members about your ideas and commit to being accountable to one another.*

- *During the coming week, ask the Holy Spirit to continue to reveal truth to you from what you've read and studied.*

- *The next lesson references a variety of verses from Proverbs. Come prepared with your Bible to explore the theme "Rich Man, Poor Man." For more in-depth lesson preparation, read chapter 7 in* Be Skillful.

Rich Man, Poor Man

(KEY VERSES: PROVERBS 1:10–19; 10:2, 4–5; 11:1; 13:11, 18, 23; 14:21, 31; 15:27; 16:16; 18:9, 11, 23; 22:29; 28:22)

Before you begin …
- *Pray for the Holy Spirit to reveal truth and wisdom as you go through this lesson.*
- *This lesson references chapter 7 in* Be Skillful. *It will be helpful for you to have your Bible and a copy of the commentary available as you work through this lesson.*

Getting Started

From the Commentary

In the book of Proverbs, King Solomon tells us a great deal about three kinds of people—the thieves, the poor who need our help, and the diligent workers. (Among the thieves, I'm including "the sluggard," the lazy person who never works but expects others to take care of him. That's being a thief, isn't it?) However, wealthy as he was (1 Kings 4; 10), King Solomon emphasized that *God's wisdom is more important than money.* "How much better

is it to get wisdom than gold! and to get understanding
rather to be chosen than silver!" (Prov. 16:16; see 2:1–5;
3:13–15; 8:10–21).

—*Be Skillful,* page 101

1. What is your first reaction to Solomon's statement that it is better to get
wisdom than gold? In what ways does popular culture uphold this proverb?
In what ways does our culture challenge it or deny it? Does the fact that
Solomon was a wealthy man add credence to the statement or weaken it?

*More to Consider: Review Matthew 6:33. How does this compare
with Solomon's teaching in Proverbs 16:16?*

2. Read this week's key verses (Prov. 1:10–19; 10:2, 4–5; 11:1; 13:11, 18,
23; 14:21, 31; 15:27; 16:16; 18:9, 11, 23; 22:29; 28:22). Which of these
verses is most meaningful to you? Explain.

Going Deeper

From the Commentary

The book of Proverbs opens with a stern warning against participating in get-rich-quick schemes that involve breaking the law (Prov. 1:10–19). These schemes are self-destructive and lead to bondage and possibly the grave. Beware of people who promise to make you wealthy without asking you to work or take any risks. "Wealth obtained by fraud dwindles, but the one who gathers by labor increases it" (13:11 NASB). "A man with an evil eye hastens after riches, and does not consider that poverty will come upon him" (28:22 NKJV). "Ill-gotten treasures are of no value, but righteousness delivers from death" (10:2 NIV).

—*Be Skillful*, page 102

3. What are some of the get-rich-quick schemes in today's world that Solomon would denounce? Why are there so many of these in our culture today? What would Solomon say about each of these shortcuts to wealth? Is a shortcut to wealth always wrong? Explain.

From the Commentary

> God demands that we be honest in all our business
> dealings. Dishonesty is robbery. "Dishonest scales are
> an abomination to the LORD, but a just weight is His
> delight" (11:1 NKJV; see 16:11; 20:10, 23). Moses com-
> manded in the law that people use honest weights and
> measures (Lev. 19:35–36; Deut. 25:13–16); since Israel
> didn't have an official Department of Standards to check
> on these things, the law wasn't always obeyed.
>
> —*Be Skillful*, page 102

4. Consider what a "just weight" looks like in business today. What are
some of the ways businesses and organizations you've worked with have
been a "delight" to the Lord (11:1)? What should our response be when we
encounter dishonest dealings? In what ways does dishonesty in business
steal even from those who aren't being dishonest? How does dishonesty
steal from families or friendships?

From the History Books

The Internet is rife with get-rich-quick schemes, nearly all of which are too good to be true because they're scams. Whether it's an advertisement from a successful motivational speaker selling his "how to be rich like me" books or an email from a Nigerian prince asking you to help him move his money out of the country, there are lots of scam artists preying on our society's hunger for wealth.

Even the church can be called into question about its practices and promises regarding wealth. Some pastors preach the "prosperity gospel" that says, in essence, "If you do these things, God will reward you with material wealth." While the Bible surely does promise blessings, it does not promise wealth to everyone who follows certain guidelines. This misleading interpretation of the true gospel is not so different from a get-rich-quick scheme.

5. If common sense says get-rich-quick schemes are scams, why do people still fall for them? How is this an example of trading wisdom for foolishness? In what ways has the church erred in dealing with the hunger for "more"? Why is the prosperity gospel no gospel at all? What wisdom is missing in those who present this as "truth"?

From the Commentary

> The sluggard *wastes God-given resources.* "He also that is slothful in his work is brother to him that is a great waster" (Prov. 18:9). The lazy person may be "working" but not doing a very good job. Consequently, what's done will either have to be thrown out or done over; this means it will cost twice as much.
>
> The sluggard also *wastes God-given opportunities.* "He who gathers in summer is a wise son; he who sleeps in harvest is a son who causes shame" (10:5 NKJV).
>
> —*Be Skillful,* page 105

6. What's the difference between someone who is a lazy worker and someone who simply isn't a very skilled worker? How can you tell the difference? How serious a sin do you think laziness is? Why?

More to Consider: Wiersbe writes in Be Skillful *that "the biggest thieves of all are the lazy people who could work but won't, the people who consume what others produce but produce nothing for others to use" (p. 103). Go through Proverbs and circle any references to "sluggards" or "slothful men" (they're mentioned at least seventeen times). Then note what Proverbs says about these people.*

From the Commentary

What are the causes of poverty and need? Some people are poor simply because they won't work. Work is available, but they prefer not to know about it. "Lazy hands make a man poor, but diligent hands bring wealth" (Prov. 10:4 NIV).

Unfortunately, some people weren't disciplined when young and taught the importance of work. "He who ignores discipline comes to poverty and shame, but whoever heeds correction is honored" (13:18 NIV). Listening to orders and obeying them, paying attention to correction and reproof and not repeating mistakes, and respecting supervision are essential to success in any job.

—*Be Skillful*, pages 106–7

7. How can you tell the difference between those who are in poverty because of circumstances out of their control and those who are in poverty because of their own choices? Does your response to poverty depend on the reason someone is poor? Why or why not? What practical answers would Solomon give to those who are suffering from the poverty of laziness? How can the church help people in this situation?

From the Commentary

> There are also times when people become poor because of *people and events over which they have no control.* "A poor man's field may produce abundant food, but injustice sweeps it away" (13:23 NIV; see 18:23; 28:8).... When there's injustice in the land and people fear the Lord, then the poor have a voice and protection from oppression.
>
> Oppressing the poor is condemned by God. "He who oppresses the poor reproaches his Maker, but he who honors Him has mercy on the needy" (Prov. 14:31 NKJV).
>
> —*Be Skillful*, page 107

8. What should the church's response be to those who have become poor because of injustice? How can the church become a voice for those suffering in poverty? In what ways does our society sometimes oppress the poor? What are some practical ways your church and community can honor God through serving the poor?

More to Consider: Read 1 Timothy 5:4, 8. What do these verses tell us about whom we're to take care of first? How does this relate to Solomon's teaching on helping the poor?

From the Commentary

> The reward for faithful hard work is—more work! "Well done, good and faithful servant; you were faithful over a few things, I will make you ruler over many things" (Matt. 25:21 NKJV; see Luke 19:16–19). "Do you see a man who excels in his work? He will stand before kings; he will not stand before unknown men" (Prov. 22:29 NKJV).
>
> One of the blessings of diligent labor is the joy of developing the kind of ability and character that others can trust, thereby fitting ourselves for the next responsibility God has prepared for us.
>
> —*Be Skillful*, page 109

9. What great responsibilities did God give David (Ps. 78:70–72)? What are other examples of increased responsibility given to someone who is diligent in work? How does this apply in the workplace? In areas of service?

From the Commentary

> If God blesses our diligent work with success, *we must be*
> *careful not to become proud.* "The wealth of the rich is their
> fortified city; they imagine it an unscalable wall" (18:11
> NIV).... If successful people aren't careful, they'll start
> mistreating people (Prov. 14:21; 18:23) and becoming a
> law to themselves (28:11).
>
> The wrong attitude toward money can *wreck friendships*
> *and even destroy a home.* "He who is greedy for gain
> troubles his own house, but he who hates bribes will live"
> (15:27 NKJV). The man or woman who thinks only of get-
> ting rich will put money ahead of people and principles,
> and soon they start to neglect the family in their frantic
> pursuit of wealth.
>
> —*Be Skillful*, pages 112–13

10. What are some ways greed has damaged the work of the church? In
what ways do successful people sometimes mistreat others (Prov. 14:21;
18:23)? Why do you think success often goes to people's heads? What is the
proper attitude to have toward money in order to avoid becoming proud?

Looking Inward

Take a moment to reflect on all that you've explored thus far in this study of "Rich Man, Poor Man." Review your notes and answers and think about how each of these things matters in your life today.

Tips for Small Groups: To get the most out of this section, form pairs or trios and have group members take turns answering these questions. Be honest and as open as you can in this discussion, but most of all, be encouraging and supportive of others. Be sensitive to those who are going through particularly difficult times and don't press for people to speak if they're uncomfortable doing so.

11. In what ways have you been tempted by get-rich-quick schemes? Have you ever tried one? What was the result? Why are you tempted by shortcuts to wealth? When you've worked hard for your money, how has that affected the way you relate to it?

12. If you've been dishonest in any business dealings, what was the underlying reason for your dishonesty? Have you made those things right? If not, what would you need to do to resolve them? If you've witnessed

others' dishonest dealings, how have you dealt with them? What are some biblically based ways to confront dishonesty in the workplace?

13. What is your emotional reaction to poverty? In what ways do you tend to judge others for their circumstances? Does it matter if the poor are poor because of their own laziness or because of circumstances out of their control? Why or why not?

Going Forward

14. Think of one or two things that you have learned that you'd like to work on in the coming week. Remember that this is all about quality, not quantity. It's better to work on one specific area of life and do it well than to work on many and do poorly (or to be so overwhelmed that you simply don't try).

Do you need to reevaluate your perspective on money? Do you need to do more for the poor? Be specific. Go back through the key verses in this lesson and put a star next to the phrase or verse that is most encouraging to you. Consider memorizing this verse.

Real-Life Application Ideas: Spend a day helping out in a homeless shelter or a similar place where the poor are offered assistance. As you serve, ask God to reveal to you the right attitude to have toward those in poverty and the right response to their need. Then act on what God says to you.

Seeking Help

15. Write a prayer below (or simply pray one in silence), inviting God to work on your mind and heart in those areas you've previously noted. Be honest about your desires and fears.

Notes for Small Groups:

- *Look for ways to put into practice the things you wrote in the Going Forward section. Talk with other group members about your ideas and commit to being accountable to one another.*

- *During the coming week, ask the Holy Spirit to continue to reveal truth to you from what you've read and studied.*

- *The next lesson references a variety of verses from Proverbs. Come prepared with your Bible to explore the theme "Family, Friends, and Neighbors." For more in-depth lesson preparation, read chapter 8 in* Be Skillful.

Family, Friends, and Neighbors

(KEY VERSES: PROVERBS 2:17; 5; 10:1; 11:9; 14:26; 19:18; 22:6, 15; 25:9–10; 27:9; 31:10–31)

Before you begin …
- *Pray for the Holy Spirit to reveal truth and wisdom as you go through this lesson.*
- *This lesson references chapter 8 in* Be Skillful. *It will be helpful for you to have your Bible and a copy of the commentary available as you work through this lesson.*

Getting Started

From the Commentary

The book of Proverbs is the best manual you'll find on people skills, because it was given to us by the God who made us, the God who can teach us what we need to know about human relationships, whether it's marriage, the family, the neighborhood, the job, or our wider circle of friends and acquaintances. If we learn and practice God's wisdom as presented in Proverbs, we'll find ourselves improving in people skills and enjoying life much more.

—*Be Skillful,* page 117

1. As you've read Proverbs, you've come across many wise sayings that are applicable to relationships. What are some of the most memorable truths you've discovered so far? Why do these appeal to you? How have you seen them lived out at home? At work? At church?

2. Read this week's key verses (Prov. 2:17; 5; 10:1; 11:9; 14:26; 19:18; 22:6, 15; 25:9–10; 27:9; 31:10–31). Which of these verses is most meaningful to you? Explain.

Going Deeper

From the Commentary

> King Solomon had seven hundred wives and three
> hundred concubines (1 Kings 11:3), and in so doing he
> disobeyed God's law—by multiplying wives (Deut. 17:17),

and by taking these wives from pagan nations that didn't worship Jehovah, the true and Living God (Ex. 34:16; Deut. 7:1–3). Eventually, these women won Solomon over to their gods, and the Lord had to discipline Solomon for his sins (1 Kings 11:4ff.).

In contrast to this, the book of Proverbs magnifies the kind of marriage that God first established in Eden: one man married to one woman for one lifetime (Gen. 2:18–25; Matt. 19:1–9). The husband is to love his wife and be faithful to her (Prov. 5). The wife is not to forsake her husband and seek her love elsewhere (2:17). They are to enjoy one another and grow in their love for each other and for the Lord.

—*Be Skillful*, page 118

3. In what ways might Solomon's experience have prepared him to speak truthfully about marriage? Why do you think he focuses on the "one man, one woman" marriage described in Genesis, despite the facts that tell us he had many wives and concubines? How does God creatively use Solomon's experience to teach us the truth about the marriage relationship?

More to Consider: In the time of the Israelites, marriages were arranged by the parents. Today, it is more typical for two people to meet and fall in love before getting married. How does today's system create unique challenges compared to couples who, in ancient days, would simply have learned to love each other over time because the decision to get married wasn't theirs in the first place?

From the Commentary

The finest description of the ideal wife is found in 31:10–31. This poem is an acrostic with the initial words of the twenty-two verses all beginning with successive letters of the Hebrew alphabet (see Ps. 119). This acrostic form was a device to help people commit the passage to memory. Perhaps Jewish parents instructed their sons and daughters to memorize this poem and use it as a guide for their lives and in their homes.

—*Be Skillful*, pages 119–20

4. What does Proverbs 31:10–31 say about the ideal wife? What are her characteristics? What is appealing about this description? What are the challenges of understanding and implementing the wisdom in this passage today? What does the rest of Proverbs tell us about what women should look for in a husband?

From Today's World

There is an ongoing conversation about the relative merits of a stay-at-home mom versus a working mom. In a time of economic uncertainty, it's not uncommon for both parents to be working full-time, and even when things are good in the economy, some moms choose to work outside the home. This can, for some, cause feelings of guilt or uncertainty in light of what is taught in Proverbs 31.

5. How does Proverbs 31 address the question of a wife's helping to provide for the family's financial well-being? Why is the idea of a working mom considered controversial to some Christians? Can working moms also pursue the ideals revealed in Proverbs 31? How, or why not?

From the Commentary

The secret of a godly woman's life is that *she fears the Lord* (31:30). It's wonderful if a wife has charm and beauty; the possession of these qualities is not a sin. But the woman who walks with the Lord and seeks to please Him has a beauty that never fades (1 Peter 3:1–6). The man who has a wife who daily reads the Word, meditates, prays, and seeks to obey God's will, has a treasure that is indeed beyond the price of rubies.

—*Be Skillful*, page 122

6. What does it mean for a woman to "fear the Lord"? What are some practical ways a wife or mom can go about pleasing God? How are these ways similar to and different from the ways a husband or dad does the same?

From the Commentary

Along with the basic necessities of physical life, what should the godly home provide for the children?

When parents walk with God, they give their children a heritage that will enrich them throughout their lives. Godliness puts beauty within the home and protection around the home. "He who fears the LORD has a secure fortress, and for his children it will be a refuge" (14:26 NIV). The world wants to penetrate that fortress and kidnap our children and grandchildren, but godly parents keep the walls strong and the spiritual weapons ready.

Every parent should pray and work so that their children will have spiritual wisdom when the time comes for them to leave the home. "A wise son makes a glad father, but a foolish son is the grief of his mother" (10:1 NKJV; see 15:20; 23:15–16, 24–25; 27:11; 29:3).

—Be Skillful, pages 123–24

7. What are the most practical ways parents can help teach their children the ways of the Lord? How do they pass along spiritual wisdom? What is the "secure fortress" available to those parents who fear the Lord (14:26)?

From the Commentary

Discipline has to do with correcting character faults in a child while there is still time to do it (22:15). Better the child is corrected by a parent than by a law enforcement officer in a correctional institution. "Chasten your son while there is hope, and do not set your heart on his destruction" (19:18 NKJV). I prefer the New International Version translation of the second clause: "do not be a willing party to his death." A vote against discipline is a vote in favor of premature death. (See 23:13–14.)

—Be Skillful, page 125

8. What does Solomon have to say about discipline in 19:18; 22:15; and 23:13–14? Why is discipline important in a Christian home? How have these verses been used to justify child abuse? What motivates some parents to impose too little discipline in their children's lives? Do you think Solomon is being overly dramatic in 23:13–14? Why or why not?

From the Commentary

Certainly it's true that children raised in the nurture and admonition of the Lord can stray from God, but they can never get away from the prayers of their parents or the seed that's been planted in their hearts. Parents should never despair but keep on praying and trusting God to bring wayward children to their senses. But that isn't what Proverbs 22:6 is speaking about. Like the other proverbs, it's not making an ironclad guarantee but is laying down a general principle.

—*Be Skillful*, page 126

9. What comfort is there in the prayers of parents when a child has lost his or her way? How can this help parents to avoid despairing? If Proverbs 22:6 isn't offering a guarantee, what is the purpose of the principle it presents?

From the Commentary

True friends know how to *keep a confidence.* "If you argue your case with a neighbor, do not betray another man's confidence, or he who hears it may shame you and you will never lose your bad reputation" (25:9–10 NIV).

This leads to the next important quality for true friends and good neighbors: *the ability to control the tongue.* "With his mouth, the godless destroys his neighbor, but through knowledge the righteous escape" (Prov. 11:9 NIV).

Faithful friends and neighbors *counsel and encourage each other.* "Ointment and perfume delight the heart, and the sweetness of a man's friend gives delight by hearty counsel" (Prov. 27:9 NKJV).

—*Be Skillful,* pages 127–29

10. What is the point of Solomon's teaching on friendships? What sorts of situations do you think prompted this wise teaching? What are some of the ways people "destroy" their neighbors with their mouths? How can faithful friends and neighbors be encouragements to each other (27:9)?

Looking Inward

Take a moment to reflect on all that you've explored thus far in this study of "Family, Friends, and Neighbors." Review your notes and answers and think about how each of these things matters in your life today.

Tips for Small Groups: To get the most out of this section, form pairs or trios and have group members take turns answering these questions. Be honest and as open as you can in this discussion, but most of all, be encouraging and supportive of others. Be sensitive to those who are going through particularly difficult times and don't press for people to speak if they're uncomfortable doing so.

11. What are some of the wise sayings from Proverbs that you've applied to your relationships? How have those truths helped your relationships? What are some of the proverbs you wish you could embrace more fully? How would you go about doing that?

12. If you are a wife, how do you react to the message of Proverbs 31? If you're a husband, what is your reaction? What are the key points in this passage that apply today? What are some of the universal truths that can apply to both married women and single women? Do you think the "Proverbs 31" woman is a good goal for women to aspire to? Why or why not?

13. If you are a parent, what are some of the ways you help teach your children in spiritual matters? What are some things you could do better? Looking back at your childhood, were you raised in the nurture of the Lord? If so, how did that help prepare you for your life in Christ today? If not, what path did God lead you down to bring you to where you are today? How can your experience help to inform a right way to raise your own children?

Going Forward

14. Think of one or two things that you have learned that you'd like to work on in the coming week. Remember that this is all about quality, not quantity. It's better to work on one specific area of life and do it well than to work on many and do poorly (or to be so overwhelmed that you simply don't try).

Do you need to address the way you interact in your marriage? Do you need to be more deliberate in how you raise your children so they might choose to follow Christ? Be specific. Go back through the key verses in this lesson and put a star next to the phrase or verse that is most encouraging to you. Consider memorizing this verse.

Real-Life Application Ideas: If you're married, seek out and make plans to attend a marriage seminar with your spouse. Use that time to grow closer together and learn how to be good encouragers to one another. If you're single, spend time exploring what Scripture has to say about romantic relationships and consider attending a singles group at your church to grow your wisdom about relationships.

Seeking Help

15. Write a prayer below (or simply pray one in silence), inviting God to work on your mind and heart in those areas you've previously noted. Be honest about your desires and fears.

Notes for Small Groups:

- *Look for ways to put into practice the things you wrote in the Going Forward section. Talk with other group members about your ideas and commit to being accountable to one another.*

- *During the coming week, ask the Holy Spirit to continue to reveal truth to you from what you've read and studied.*

- *The next lesson references a variety of verses from Proverbs. Come prepared with your Bible to explore the theme "Speaking of Life and Death." For more in-depth lesson preparation, read chapter 9 in* Be Skillful.

Speaking of Life and Death

(KEY VERSES: PROVERBS 4:7; 8:6–8; 10:13; 12:19, 22; 15:1, 4, 7, 18; 16:1, 21; 18:21; 19:21; 25:12, 18; 26:21; 28:23; 29:22)

Before you begin …
- *Pray for the Holy Spirit to reveal truth and wisdom as you go through this lesson.*
- *This lesson references chapter 9 in* Be Skillful. *It will be helpful for you to have your Bible and a copy of the commentary available as you work through this lesson.*

Getting Started

From the Commentary

"Death and life are in the power of the tongue" (Prov. 18:21).

When you summarize what Proverbs teaches about human speech, you end up with four important propositions: (1) speech is an awesome gift from God; (2) speech can be used to do good; (3) speech can be used to do evil;

and (4) only God can help us use the gift of speech for good.

—*Be Skillful,* page 133

1. Is Proverbs 18:21 overstating the power of words? Why or why not? Why do words have so much power? What does this say about the Creator of words? Read John 1. How does John's portrayal of "the Word" add insight to the message of Proverbs 18:21?

More to Consider: Read James 3:5–8. How does this passage support the message in Proverbs 18:21?

2. Read this week's key verses (Prov. 4:7; 8:6–8; 10:13; 12:19, 22; 15:1, 4, 7, 18; 16:1, 21; 18:21; 19:21; 25:12, 18; 26:21; 28:23; 29:22). Which of these verses is most meaningful to you? Explain.

Going Deeper

From the Commentary

> Right words are like *nourishing, health-giving food.* "The
> tongue that brings healing is a tree of life, but a deceitful
> tongue crushes the spirit" (15:4 NIV). What a wonderful
> thing it is to say the right words and help to heal a broken
> spirit! The phrase "tree of life" means "source of life" and
> goes back to Genesis 2:9.
>
> The apostle Paul considered biblical doctrine to be
> "healthy doctrine" ("sound doctrine," KJV) that nourishes
> the believer's spiritual life. He warned Timothy to beware
> of anything that was "contrary to sound [healthy] doc-
> trine" (1 Tim. 1:10), and he reminded him that the time
> would come when professed Christians wouldn't "endure
> sound [healthy] doctrine" (2 Tim. 4:3).
>
> —*Be Skillful*, page 135

3. What are some good examples of "right words" that can heal? Where do
you see this being lived out in church? In the family? At work? How can
words actually contribute to healing someone's spirit?

From the Commentary

> Our words can bring peace instead of war. "A soft [gentle] answer turns away wrath, but a harsh word stirs up anger" (Prov. 15:1 NKJV). "A hot-tempered man stirs up dissension, but a patient man calms a quarrel" (v. 18 NIV). Solomon isn't advising us to compromise the truth and say that what's wrong is really right. Rather, he's counseling us to have a gentle spirit and a conciliatory attitude when we disagree with others.
>
> —*Be Skillful*, page 136

4. When have you seen harsh words stir up anger? As you look at the major conflicts in your family of origin, your workplace, or other relationships, what role have words played? What is the difference between patience and sweeping conflict under the rug?

From Today's World

Before the advent of phones, text messaging, and email, conversations between two people occurred either face-to-face or in letters. Today, many conversations are recorded in some form, and some are even broadcast to a larger audience across the Internet. Words that could have been spoken in anger, then quickly regretted in an apology, have a longer shelf-life. All people, but particularly those who hold public office or are in the public eye, have to be aware that everything they say could come back to haunt them at a later date.

5. Words have the power to heal and to hurt. How does today's technology enhance both of those truths? What makes conversation today more challenging in light of the fact that words aren't spoken once, then forgotten? What new wisdom must we employ in order to avoid causing unnecessary pain when speaking out on a subject or about an individual? Find a proverb or create one that might apply to today's world of fast-paced, always-accessible communication and write that here.

From the Commentary

Our words can help restore those who have sinned. "As an earring of gold, and an ornament of fine gold, so is a wise reprover upon an obedient [listening] ear" (Prov. 25:12). It isn't easy to reprove those who are wrong, and we need to do it in a meek and loving spirit (Gal. 6:1); yet it must be done. To flatter those who are disobeying God's Word will only confirm them in their sin and make us their accomplices. "He who rebukes a man will find more favor afterward than he who flatters with the tongue" (Prov. 28:23 NKJV).

—*Be Skillful*, page 137

6. What are some examples of words that help to restore someone who has sinned (25:12)? What does this tell us about the spiritual responsibility God has given us by giving us the gift of words? What is a proper way to use words to reprove or rebuke someone (28:23)? What common mistakes do people make when trying to do this? What role does the Holy Spirit play in our attempts to restore those who have sinned?

From the Commentary

Our words can instruct the ignorant. "The lips of the wise disperse knowledge" (Prov. 15:7). "The wise in heart are called discerning, and pleasant words promote instruction" (16:21 NIV). While there are many good and helpful things to learn in this brief life that we have on earth, the most important is the wisdom of God found in the Word of God (8:6–8). "Wisdom is the principal thing;

therefore get wisdom. And in all your getting, get understanding" (4:7 NKJV). After we acquire wisdom, we must share it with others, for "wisdom is found on the lips of the discerning" (10:13 NIV).

—*Be Skillful*, pages 137–38

7. Think of examples from your experience that illustrate the truth that words can instruct. If you were the person being instructed, how did these words help you? If you were the teacher, how did you help others to learn? How do you "get understanding" (4:7)? Who are some of the discerning people in your church? Your community?

From the Commentary

We hurt others by lying. "Truthful lips endure forever, but a lying tongue lasts only a moment" (Prov. 12:19 NIV). "Lying lips are an abomination to the LORD, but they that deal truly are his delight" (12:22; see 6:16–17).… When words can't be trusted, then society starts to fall apart. Contracts are useless, promises are vain, the judicial system becomes a farce, and all personal relationships

are suspect. "Like a club or a sword or a sharp arrow is
the man who gives false testimony against his neighbor"
(25:18 NIV).

—Be Skillful, page 140

8. What makes lying such a temptation for us? In what ways do a "lying
tongue last a moment" and truthful lips "endure forever" (12:19)? Can you
think of an example that underscores the unraveling power of lies? How
can dishonesty damage an entire system or government? A business? A
family? What are some practical ways to avoid the temptation to fall into
falsehood?

*More to Consider: Read Leviticus 19:16. How does this passage
support the ideas about speech that are being presented in Proverbs?
What are the negative consequences of being a "talebearer"?*

From the Commentary

> We hurt others by speaking in anger. "An angry man stirs up dissension, and a hot-tempered one commits many sins" (29:22 NIV). Angry people keep adding fuel to the fire (26:21) instead of trying to find ways to put the fire out. Many people carry anger in their hearts while they outwardly pretend to be at peace with their friends, and they cover their anger with hypocritical words. If we're inwardly angry at people, all our profuse professions of friendship are but a thin veneer over common clay.
>
> —*Be Skillful*, page 142

9. In what ways do angry words "stir up dissension"? How do angry people add fuel to the fire (26:21)? How does even our unexpressed anger affect our relationships? If something or someone causes us to be angry, what is a proper, biblical response to that anger?

From the Commentary

> Proverbs 16:1 has been a great help to me, especially when
> I've been called upon to give counsel: "To man belong the
> plans of the heart, but from the LORD comes the reply of
> the tongue" (NIV). When you couple this with 19:21, it
> gives you great encouragement: "Many are the plans in
> a man's heart, but it is the LORD's purpose that prevails"
> (NIV). On many occasions, I've had to make decisions
> about complex matters, and the Lord has given me just
> the words to speak. However, if my heart had not been in
> touch with His Word and yielded to His will, the Spirit
> might not have been able to direct me. If we make our
> plans the best we can and commit them to the Lord, He'll
> guide us in what we say and do.
>
> —*Be Skillful*, pages 143–44

10. Where do we go to find the Lord's purpose for our lives? What does
it look like in practical terms to be in touch with God's Word? How does
being in touch with God's Word help us to yield to His will? How can we
learn to live out the truth of Proverbs 16:1 in relationship to those close
to us? To casual friends and strangers? To people we don't get along with?

Looking Inward

Take a moment to reflect on all that you've explored thus far in this study of "Speaking of Life and Death." Review your notes and answers and think about how each of these things matters in your life today.

Tips for Small Groups: To get the most out of this section, form pairs or trios and have group members take turns answering these questions. Be honest and as open as you can in this discussion, but most of all, be encouraging and supportive of others. Be sensitive to those who are going through particularly difficult times and don't press for people to speak if they're uncomfortable doing so.

11. What are some examples in your own life of the dangerous power of negative words? If you were the recipient of these words, how did they affect you? If you were the speaker, how did they impact the recipient? Is it easy for you to control your tongue? Why or why not? What are some simple steps you can take to avoid wielding words as weapons?

12. Who are some of the people in your life who have given you "healing" words? What was the circumstance that prompted their words? Think

about times when you've offered similar healing words to others. What role did the Holy Spirit play in helping you to respond to the need at hand?

13. When are you most tempted to lie? Why is this such a temptation for you? What potential damage could this lying cause? How can you work to overcome this temptation and instead speak the truth? What does it mean to speak the truth "in love" to someone? How can doing this have a lasting, positive impact on you and the person to whom you're speaking?

Going Forward

14. Think of one or two things that you have learned that you'd like to work on in the coming week. Remember that this is all about quality, not quantity. It's better to work on one specific area of life and do it well than to work on many and do poorly (or to be so overwhelmed that you simply don't try).

Do you need to work on avoiding negative speech? Do you need to find the strength to speak the truth when tempted to lie? Be specific. Go back through the key verses in this lesson and put a star next to the phrase or verse that is most encouraging to you. Consider memorizing this verse.

Real-Life Application Ideas: Do a little research on the power of words in history and today. Review the root causes of wars to determine just how much of what sparked the conflict was based on words. Then skim the news for stories illustrating the dangers of today's social media and how words spoken out of frustration or anger can negatively affect someone's livelihood. Talk with a friend about your findings, and pray for wisdom and strength to avoid using words that damage others or yourself.

Seeking Help

15. Write a prayer below (or simply pray one in silence), inviting God to work on your mind and heart in those areas you've previously noted. Be honest about your desires and fears.

Notes for Small Groups:

- *Look for ways to put into practice the things you wrote in the Going Forward section. Talk with other group members about your ideas and commit to being accountable to one another.*

- *During the coming week, ask the Holy Spirit to continue to reveal truth to you from what you've read and studied.*

- *The next lesson references a variety of verses from Proverbs. Come prepared with your Bible to explore the theme "God's Guidance." For more in-depth lesson preparation, read chapters 10–11 in* Be Skillful.

God's Guidance
(KEY VERSES: PROVERBS 2:13, 18, 20; 3:1, 5–6; 6:20; 7:1; 8:20; 12:15, 28; 20:18; 21:2; 27:8; 30:5)

Before you begin …
- *Pray for the Holy Spirit to reveal truth and wisdom as you go through this lesson.*
- *This lesson references chapters 10–11 in* Be Skillful. *It will be helpful for you to have your Bible and a copy of the commentary available as you work through this lesson.*

Getting Started

From the Commentary

Those who obey the wisdom taught in God's Word will become more skillful in handling the affairs of life. But we must not think that this wisdom is a set of rules or a collection of "success formulas" that anyone can occasionally apply as he or she pleases. Following God's wisdom is a full-time endeavor.... If you're concerned with making a *life*, you must major on building godly character.

This explains why the words *righteous* and *righteousness* are used so often in Proverbs. Wisdom leads "in the way of righteousness" (8:20), and "in the way of righteousness is life" (12:28).

The Hebrew words in Proverbs that are translated "righteous," "righteousness," "upright," and "uprightness" describe ethical conduct that conforms to God's standards and moral character that comes from a right relationship to the Lord and His Word. True righteousness isn't just toeing the line and obeying the rules. As Jesus teaches in the Sermon on the Mount, it is possible for us to obey the law outwardly while cultivating sin inwardly. It isn't enough for us not to kill or not to commit adultery; we must also not harbor hatred and lust in our hearts (Matt. 5:21–48).

—*Be Skillful,* pages 149–50

1. In what ways is following God's wisdom a full-time endeavor? What is the "way of righteousness" that Solomon refers to in Proverbs 8:20? What does it mean to walk in the way of righteousness? How does listening to God's instruction help us walk this path?

More to Consider: Read Proverbs 8:6, 8–9 and Psalm 119:138. What do these passages say about God's Word? What do they tell us about how we ought to respond to God's words?

2. Read this week's key verses (Prov. 2:13, 18, 20; 3:1, 5–6; 6:20; 7:1; 8:20; 12:15, 28; 20:18; 21:2; 27:8; 30:5). Which of these verses is most meaningful to you? Explain.

Going Deeper

From the Commentary

It is unthinkable that a righteous God would violate His own nature and disobey His own Word by asking His people to be less than righteous. Before He gave Israel His law, God said, "Now therefore, if you will indeed obey My voice and keep My covenant, then you shall be a special treasure to Me above all people ... and you shall be to Me a kingdom of priests and a holy nation" (Ex. 19:5–6 NKJV).

The problem, of course, is that people are—people. And that means that they're sinners. "Every way of a man is

right in his own eyes, but the LORD weighs the hearts"
(Prov. 21:2 NKJV).

—*Be Skillful*, page 151

3. Why do so many people believe they know "the right way" to live
and don't need input from outside? How does this arrogance affect our
relationship with others? With God? If only God knows the right way,
how are we to know when someone is teaching God's way and not his or
her own? What are the markers that help us to know what is God's truth?

From the Commentary

In our study of Proverbs 2—4, we learned that following
the way of wisdom is compared to a pilgrim walking a
path. As we follow His wisdom, God protects, directs,
and perfects our path. God's desire for us is that we "walk
in the way of goodness, and keep to the paths of righteousness" (2:20 NKJV).

—*Be Skillful*, page 153

4. Generally speaking, who are some of the evil men who "walk in the ways of darkness" (2:13) or the evil women whose "house leads down to death" (2:18) in the world today? Why do people leave the paths of righteousness in the first place? What draws them from the righteous path?

From Today's World

As the lines between traditional media and social media are blurred, and the Internet becomes a place of equal access for the wise and the foolish, determining what is good and what is evil can be challenging for those who don't already know and trust God's Word. Pools of information with varying reliability and "wisdom" offered by celebrities whose only claim on the public ear is their celebrity status mean it is getting to be more and more difficult to sort through information in search of truth.

5. How do the challenges of this Internet age affect the manner in which we seek out answers to questions, big and small? What are some of the greater concerns this access to information poses? How does this impact the way we are to raise our children or teach others? How do we go about testing the information we find online and elsewhere against God's Word? In what ways can these new technologies actually help us discover true wisdom?

From the Commentary

> "Like a bird that strays from its nest is a man who strays from his home" (27:8 NIV). In our contemporary American society, about 17 percent of the population relocates each year, but in ancient Israel, people stayed close to home. The extended family was the norm, with children and grandchildren learning to revere their ancestors and respectfully learning from them. The person who strayed from home was either up to no good or had to leave because of family problems.

> But the verse applies spiritually as well as geographically: We must not stray from the example of our godly ancestors or the spiritual treasures they left us.

> —*Be Skillful*, page 157

6. Why are people so nomadic today? What are the disadvantages of a transient life? What does it mean, metaphorically, to "stray from home"? How can we become spiritually grounded in a home? In what ways is our spiritual grounding a better definition of "home" than the house we live in?

From the Commentary

No matter how we may feel personally about the topic, if we're going to be skillful in life, we have to understand what God's will is and how it works in our everyday experiences. In the book of Proverbs, Solomon shares with us the essentials for knowing, doing, and enjoying the will of God.

The first of these is faith.

"Trust in the LORD with all your heart, and lean not on your own understanding; in all your ways acknowledge Him, and He shall direct your paths" (Prov. 3:5–6 NKJV). These two verses have encouraged believers everywhere in their quest for God's guidance, and for those who have sincerely met the conditions, the promise has never failed.

—*Be Skillful*, pages 163–64

7. What does it mean to "trust in the Lord"? How do believers go about trusting "with all their heart"? Why is our own understanding not enough?

From the Commentary

> In the book of Proverbs, the wise father repeatedly gives
> his son loving calls to obedience. "My son, do not forget
> my law, but let your heart keep my commands" (3:1
> NKJV). "My son, keep your father's command, and do not
> forsake the law of your mother" (6:20 NKJV). "My son,
> keep my words, and treasure my commands within you"
> (7:1 NKJV). *The will of God isn't a curiosity for us to study,*
> *it's a command for us to obey; God isn't obligated to reveal*
> *His will unless we're willing to do it.*
>
> —*Be Skillful,* page 166

8. What does Wiersbe mean when he writes, "The will of God isn't a
curiosity for us to study"? What keeps us from being willing to do what
God says? What helps us become willing? What do you learn from Proverbs
that motivates you to be willing?

More to Consider: The Hebrew word for "acknowledge" in Proverbs
3:6 is the same word used to describe the marriage relationship

in Genesis 4:1. How does this shed light on the deeper meaning of Proverbs 3:6?

From the Commentary

> In order to "trust in the Lord," we must have His Word to instruct us, because "faith comes by hearing, and hearing by the word of God" (Rom. 10:17 NKJV). Scripture is "the word of faith" (Rom. 10:8) that generates and nourishes faith in our hearts, and we can depend on His Word. "Every word of God is pure; He is a shield to those who put their trust in Him" (Prov. 30:5 NKJV; see 22:17–21).
>
> —*Be Skillful*, page 167

9. If faith comes by "hearing, and hearing by the word of God" (Rom. 10:17), what are some practical ways Christians can hear the Word of God? How important is regular Bible study to developing our faith? In what ways are God's words "shields" to those who trust Him (Prov. 30:5)? How can those shields help us in daily life?

From the Commentary

> "Plans are established by counsel; by wise counsel wage war" (Prov. 20:18 NKJV). If experienced generals seek counsel as they wage war, shouldn't we seek counsel for the battles of life? It's dangerous to rely on our own wisdom and experience and to ignore the wisdom and experience of other believers who have successfully walked with the Lord. "The way of a fool is right in his own eyes, but he who heeds counsel is wise" (12:15 NKJV).
>
> —*Be Skillful*, pages 168–69

10. What are some of the different ways Christians can seek wise counsel? (See Prov. 23:33; 27:6, 9.) How do people isolate themselves? Why? What are some of the ways the church can help those who tend to isolate themselves from wise counsel?

Looking Inward

Take a moment to reflect on all that you've explored thus far in this study of "God's Guidance." Review your notes and answers and think about how each of these things matters in your life today.

Tips for Small Groups: To get the most out of this section, form pairs or trios and have group members take turns answering these questions. Be honest and as open as you can in this discussion, but most of all, be encouraging and supportive of others. Be sensitive to those who are going through particularly difficult times and don't press for people to speak if they're uncomfortable doing so.

11. What are some of the ways you regularly seek God's wisdom? How do you differentiate between the wisdom of the world and that which comes from God? What resources do you have to help you in this endeavor?

12. In what ways are you transient in your life? What causes you to feel this way? How can the foundation of God's wisdom help you feel grounded? What are some practical ways you can build that foundation?

13. How much time do you spend regularly in God's Word? Do you find it easy or difficult to make time for this study? Explain. How do you know if your Bible-study time has become a ritual instead of a meaningful time of hearing God speak? What are some ways to stay fresh and open to God in your study time?

Going Forward

14. Think of one or two things that you have learned that you'd like to work on in the coming week. Remember that this is all about quality, not quantity. It's better to work on one specific area of life and do it well than to work on many and do poorly (or to be so overwhelmed that you simply don't try).

Do you need to do something about your tendency to be nomadic and isolated? Do you need to reevaluate your Bible-study habits? Be specific.

Go back through the key verses in this lesson and put a star next to the phrase or verse that is most encouraging to you. Consider memorizing this verse.

> *Real-Life Application Ideas: If you don't already have time set aside for regular Bible study, consider what sort of system would work best for you. Perhaps first thing in the morning is a good time for reading and hearing God speak through His Word. Or maybe just before bed. As you think about your Bible-study habits, consider also how to approach the Bible with a desire to learn instead of a sense of obligation. Don't guilt yourself for not reading an hour every day if that's not the best way for you to grow good study habits. Spend time in prayer, asking God to help you make good choices for study, then trust the Holy Spirit to guide you in this path.*

Seeking Help

15. Write a prayer below (or simply pray one in silence), inviting God to work on your mind and heart in those areas you've previously noted. Be honest about your desires and fears.

Notes for Small Groups:

- *Look for ways to put into practice the things you wrote in the Going Forward section. Talk with other group members about your ideas and commit to being accountable to one another.*

- *During the coming week, ask the Holy Spirit to continue to reveal truth to you from what you've read and studied.*

- *The next lesson references a variety of verses from Proverbs. Come prepared with your Bible to explore the theme "Familiar Sins." For more in-depth lesson preparation, read chapter 12 in* Be Skillful.

Familiar Sins
(KEY VERSES: PROVERBS 6:16–17; 15:25; 16:18; 18:12; 20:1; 21:17, 24; 23:20–21, 29–35; 30:11–14, 17)

Before you begin …
- *Pray for the Holy Spirit to reveal truth and wisdom as you go through this lesson.*
- *This lesson references chapter 12 in* Be Skillful. *It will be helpful for you to have your Bible and a copy of the commentary available as you work through this lesson.*

Getting Started

From the Commentary

Thanks to worldwide media coverage and the constant pressure for higher program ratings, sin has become an important part of international entertainment. Evil activities that we ought to be weeping over are now sources of entertainment; they are vividly displayed on movie and TV screens and discussed in depth in newspapers and magazines. The all-seeing camera moves into the bedroom, the barroom, and the courtroom and enables excited viewers to enjoy sin vicariously. Movies and TV are instructing generation after generation of children how to ridicule virginity, laugh at sobriety, challenge authority, and reject honesty.

The book of Proverbs has something to say about popular sins that are weakening our homes, threatening the peace of our communities, and destroying lives.

—*Be Skillful,* page 177

1. Based solely on what you've read in Proverbs so far, how do Solomon's words speak to today's "popular" sins? In what ways is Proverbs a timeless response to a modern problem? What does this say about the nature of sin? About God's challenge to believers living in a sin-filled world?

More to Consider: Proverbs has some stern warnings about drunkenness. What do you think prompted such a strong series of statements? What might Solomon say to modern culture today about this particular popular sin?

2. Read this week's key verses (Prov. 6:16–17; 15:25; 16:18; 18:12; 20:1; 21:17, 24; 23:20–21, 29–35; 30:11–14, 17). Which of these verses is most meaningful to you? Explain.

Going Deeper

From the Commentary

"Wine is a mocker, strong drink is a brawler, and whoever is led astray by it is not wise" (Prov. 20:1 NKJV). This is the first of several passages in Proverbs that warn against what today we call "alcohol abuse." Alcohol mocks people by creating in them a thirst for more while not satisfying that thirst. The more people drink, the less they enjoy it. The drinker becomes a drunk and then a brawler. In spite of what the slick advertising says about the charm of drink, it just isn't a smart thing to do. As a Japanese proverb puts it, "First the man takes a drink; then the drink takes a drink; then the drink takes the man."

—*Be Skillful*, pages 178–79

3. What makes alcohol abuse such a common problem in America today? What role does advertising play in this? What are some wise ways to combat the media and cultural onslaught that says "drinking is fun" or "drinking makes you cool"? Why is this a difficult battle in today's society?

From the Commentary

Addiction to alcohol can lead to poverty (21:17), so it's wise to stay away from the people who encourage you to drink (23:20–21). Proverbs 23:29–35 is the most vivid description of the tragic consequences of drunkenness you will find anywhere in Scripture.

—*Be Skillful*, page 179

4. Go through Proverbs 23:29–35 and circle all the consequences of drunkenness. Why don't people who suffer these consequences turn away from drinking? In what ways can they become slaves to drink? How does being a slave to drink affect a person's ability to seek and serve God?

From Today's World

A few decades ago, TV stopped airing advertisements for cigarettes. Many television shows even stopped depicting people smoking as the public concern over the health dangers of smoking grew louder than the murmur of those who were fans of cigarettes. Though the dangers of drinking alcohol are different from those of smoking, there has been little if no outcry from the public to reduce the number or frequency of advertisements for alcoholic beverages. In fact, many of the most-watched commercials nestled in among the Super Bowl are for alcoholic beverages. Despite simple disclaimers about "drinking responsibly" that often accompany the advertising, drinking is certainly glamorized in ads. Science has even entered the conversation, offering medical evidence of the health benefits of drinking a glass of red wine a day, for example.

5. What is a proper Christian response to the way our culture depicts drinking? How are Solomon's words still applicable today? What is at the core of Solomon's concerns? How can we respond to that core concern in practical ways?

More to Consider: The New Testament warns today's Christians about the sin of drunkenness (Rom. 13:13; see also 1 Thess. 5:7; Luke 21:34). Galatians 5:21 names drunkenness as one of the works of the flesh, and 1 Peter 2:11 admonishes us to "abstain from sinful desires, which war against your soul." How does our culture today impact the way Christians view this sin?

From the Commentary

"The eye that mocks his father, and scorns obedience to his mother, the ravens of the valley will pick it out, and the young eagles will eat it" (Prov. 30:17 NKJV). The child who looks at his or her parents with contempt and disrespect will one day be treated like an unburied corpse, and to be left unburied was a great reproach in Israel. As I read the newspapers and news magazines, I become more and more convinced that we're living in the generation described in Proverbs 30:11–14 with its pride, greed, violence, and lack of appreciation for parents.

—*Be Skillful*, page 182

6. Proverbs 30:11–14 describes an ugly society. In what ways do you see this ugliness played out in modern culture? Why do you think Solomon uses such bold language in Proverbs 30? What does this say about the condition of the culture he was initially addressing? What does this truth say today about the universal foibles and sins of humankind? About the timelessness of God's wisdom?

From the Commentary

Wise people believe God's truth and live for reality and not for illusion. "The wisdom of the prudent is to give thought to their ways, but the folly of fools is deception" (Prov. 14:8 NIV). Some of the deceptive illusions people are foolishly clinging to today are:

"There are no consequences, so do as you please."

"If it feels good, it is good."

"The important thing in life is to have fun."

"There are no absolutes."

—*Be Skillful*, page 183

7. What are other examples of "deceptive illusions" that people are clinging to today? What makes these "deceptions"? What makes them so attractive?

From the Commentary

> God calls covetousness idolatry (Eph. 5:5; Col. 3:5) because a covetous heart puts something else in the place that God rightfully should occupy in our lives. But the modern business society applauds covetousness and calls it "ambition" and "the first step to success." Business magazines praise the "pyramid climbers" who get to the top, no matter how they got there.
>
> —*Be Skillful*, page 184

8. Read Proverbs 15:27 and 27:20. What do these verses say about greed? How is the topic of greed addressed by popular American culture? How has it invaded the church? What are the greatest dangers of a culture that is defined by greed?

From the Commentary

> Many theologians believe that pride is the "sin of all sins," for it was pride that changed an angel into the Devil (Isa. 14:12–15). Lucifer's "I will be like the most high" (v. 14)

challenged the very throne of God; in the garden of Eden, it became, "You will be like God" (Gen. 3:5 NKJV). Eve believed it, and you know the rest of the story. "Glory to man in the highest" is the rallying cry of proud, godless humanity that's still defying God and trying to build heaven on earth (11:1–9; Rev. 18).

"The proud and arrogant man—'Mocker' is his name; he behaves with overweening pride" (Prov. 21:24 NIV). "Before his downfall a man's heart is proud, but humility comes before honor" (18:12 NIV; see 29:23). God hates "a proud look" (6:16–17) and promises to destroy the house of the proud (15:25). Just about every Christian can quote Proverbs 16:18, but not all of us heed it: "Pride goes before destruction, and a haughty spirit before a fall" (NKJV).

—*Be Skillful*, pages 185–86

9. Why is pride such a dangerous sin? Think of some of the greater missteps in our culture and even in the church. What role, if any, did pride play in those situations? What are some things we can do to avoid becoming prideful? What role does the wise counsel of friends play?

From the Commentary

> The five "popular sins" I've discussed—drunkenness, disrespect, illusion, greed, and pride—have been with mankind since the days of the flood, but for some reason, they seem to be even more prevalent today. Perhaps it's because the news coverage is better. Or maybe it's because we're in the last days. We expect to find these sins prevalent among lost people, but we don't expect to find them in the church. If the church ever hopes to witness to the lost world, it must be different from the lost world.
>
> —*Be Skillful*, page 187

10. Why do you think the five sins noted in this week's study persist today? What does this say about our "fallen" nature? What does this say about humankind's continuing need for salvation? How can the church respond in positive ways to a world beset by these sins?

Looking Inward

Take a moment to reflect on all that you've explored thus far in this study of "Familiar Sins." Review your notes and answers and think about how each of these things matters in your life today.

Tips for Small Groups: To get the most out of this section, form pairs or trios and have group members take turns answering these questions. Be honest and as open as you can in this discussion, but most of all, be encouraging and supportive of others. Be sensitive to those who are going through particularly difficult times and don't press for people to speak if they're uncomfortable doing so.

11. Think about the popular sins noted in this week's study. Which of these is most difficult for you to avoid? Why are these sins so tempting for you? What are some examples of times you've overcome the temptation to fall into sin? How can you continue to work on beating that temptation?

12. What thoughts do you have about Proverbs' focus on the sin of drunkenness? Are things different today? Why or why not? How does your opinion on alcohol affect the way you view this particular sin? While it is clear that the Bible doesn't condone drunkenness, some might argue that it

encourages or allows for drinking alcohol. What is your view on this? How can you support your view biblically?

13. Describe your greatest struggle with pride. Why is this such a struggle for you? What are some practical things you can do to keep from falling into the trap of pride?

Going Forward

14. Think of one or two things that you have learned that you'd like to work on in the coming week. Remember that this is all about quality, not quantity. It's better to work on one specific area of life and do it well than to work on many and do poorly (or to be so overwhelmed that you simply don't try).

Do you need to reconsider your opinion on drinking alcohol? Do you need to pray for guidance to avoid the "popular sins" you struggle with? Be specific. Go back through the key verses in this lesson and put a star next to the phrase or verse that is most encouraging to you. Consider memorizing this verse.

Real-Life Application Ideas: Use the media's fascination with alcohol to invite thoughtful discussion with your family and friends about a godly perspective on drinking and drunkenness. While watching TV together or after seeing a movie, set time aside to talk about how drinking is depicted and how that lines up or contradicts God's wisdom on the subject. You can do this with the other "popular sins" as well. During this time, seek to understand rather than start arguments. Pray before you talk and ask God to show you His truth in the course of your conversation.

Seeking Help

15. Write a prayer below (or simply pray one in silence), inviting God to work on your mind and heart in those areas you've previously noted. Be honest about your desires and fears.

Notes for Small Groups:

- *Look for ways to put into practice the things you wrote in the Going Forward section. Talk with other group members about your ideas and commit to being accountable to one another.*

- *During the coming week, ask the Holy Spirit to continue to reveal truth to you from what you've read and studied.*

- *The next lesson references a variety of verses from Proverbs. Come prepared with your Bible to explore the theme "Our God." For more in-depth lesson preparation, read chapter 13 in* Be Skillful.

Our God

(KEY VERSES: PROVERBS 2:6–7; 3:5–6, 19–20; 5:21; 9:10; 14:31; 15:3; 16:4, 9; 19:21; 21:2, 12; 22:2; 24:11–12; 30:3)

Before you begin …
- *Pray for the Holy Spirit to reveal truth and wisdom as you go through this lesson.*
- *This lesson references chapter 13 in* Be Skillful. *It will be helpful for you to have your Bible and a copy of the commentary available as you work through this lesson.*

Getting Started

From the Commentary

We study the Word of God so that we might better know the God of the Word. The better acquainted we are with God, the more we become like Him and acquire the skills we need for life and service. "The fear of the LORD is the beginning of wisdom, and the knowledge of the Holy One is understanding" (Prov. 9:10 NKJV). You can make a living without knowing many things, but you can't make a life without knowing God.

If we read the book of Proverbs, or any book in the Bible, seeking only for doctrinal truth but ignoring God Himself, we'll miss what the Holy Spirit wants to say to us and do for us. It would be like a child devoting hours to studying the family album but not spending time with his family, getting to know them personally.

—*Be Skillful,* page 191

1. Respond to this statement: "You can make a living without knowing many things, but you can't make a life without knowing God." How does Proverbs 9:10 support this statement? How can people study Proverbs (or any book of the Bible) and still miss out on knowing God? What is the key to finding true understanding in Scripture?

More to Consider: A. W. Tozer wrote, "It is impossible to keep our moral practices sound and our inward attitudes right while our idea of God is erroneous or inadequate." What is your initial reaction to this statement? What are some of the ways Proverbs adds to our "right understanding" of God?

2. Read this week's key verses (Prov. 2:6–7; 3:5–6, 19–20; 5:21; 9:10; 14:31; 15:3; 16:4, 9; 19:21; 21:2, 12; 22:2; 24:11–12; 30:3). Which of these verses is most meaningful to you? Explain.

Going Deeper

From the Commentary

> According to Proverbs 9:10 and 30:3, God is "the Holy One" (NKJV); the word translated "holy" means "utterly different, wholly other." God's very nature is holy: "You shall be holy, for I am holy" (Lev. 11:44–45 NKJV; 19:2; 20:7, 26; 21:8, 15; 22:9, 16, 32; 1 Peter 1:16). "God is light and in him is no darkness at all" (1 John 1:5).
>
> But we must not think of God's holiness simply as the absence of defilement, like a sterilized surgical instrument. Nor is God's holiness an inert, negative attribute. It's something positive and active, His perfect nature accomplishing His perfect will.

Proverbs 21:12 calls God "the Righteous One" (NIV) or "the righteous God" (NKJV) and states that He judges the wicked for their wickedness. A holy God must be righteous in all His ways and just in all His dealings (24:11–12).

—*Be Skillful*, pages 192–93

3. In what ways is God's holiness an active thing? Where do God's children intersect with His holiness on a regular basis? Why must a holy God be righteous (24:11–12)?

From the Commentary

The fact that God is holy and just assures us that there are righteous principles that govern the universe and His dealings with us. As Dr. A. T. Pierson put it, "History is His story." "The LORD works out everything for his own ends—even the wicked for a day of disaster" (Prov. 16:4 NIV). "Many are the plans in a man's heart, but it is the LORD's purpose that prevails" (19:21 NIV). The Christian believer remembers Colossians 1:16: "All things were created by him [Christ], and for him." Jesus Christ is the Alpha and the Omega, the beginning and the end of all things.

—*Be Skillful*, page 193

4. Why is it important for us to know that there will be a day of reckoning for the wicked (16:4)? If all things were created by Christ and for Him, what implications does this have for the way we live out our lives in the everyday?

From Today's World

For many people, the "big bang" theory is an idea worth fighting for. This idea that the universe simply came to exist out of nothing is an important pivot point for supporting the theory of evolution. Science continues to seek answers to the origin of the universe, even as it sets forth the current ideas as factual. Meanwhile, Christians who believe God had something to do with the creation of the universe find themselves at odds with the world's scientific theories.

5. How does the theory of the "big bang" affect a person's belief about his or her purpose in life? How does God's role in creation give each of us

meaning and purpose? What are some ways we can see the fingerprints of God in our physical world? Why are so many people unwilling to see God's role and instead, consider the very act of existence itself to be an accident?

More to Consider: Wiersbe writes, "Divine sovereignty doesn't destroy human responsibility and turn humans into robots" (p. 194). What is your response to this statement? How can human responsibility and God's sovereignty both exist at the same time?

From the Commentary

The sovereignty of God is one of the greatest motivations for Christian life and service, because *we know that God is on the throne and controls all things.* His commandments are His enablements, and "we know that all things work together for good to those who love God, to those who are the called according to His purpose" (Rom. 8:28 NKJV). Instead of being a deterrent to evangelism, an under-standing of divine sovereignty is a stimulus to biblical evangelism; for we are sure that God is "taking out" a "people for His name" (Acts 15:14 NKJV; see 18:1–11).

As sovereign Ruler over all things, the Lord sees and knows what's happening, the thoughts, actions, words, and motives of all people. "For a man's ways are in full view of the LORD, and he examines all his paths" (Prov. 5:21 NIV). "The eyes of the LORD are everywhere, keeping watch on the wicked and the good" (15:3 NIV). "The LORD weighs the hearts" (21:2 NKJV; see 17:3; 24:12). When God judges, He judges justly, whether He's punishing the wicked or rewarding the righteous.

It's encouraging to know that "the LORD reigns" (Ps. 93:1 NKJV) and that His righteous purposes will be fulfilled.

— *Be Skillful*, pages 194–95

6. The concept of God's sovereignty can be difficult to grasp. To some it might even seem more like the role of *1984*'s Big Brother than our loving Father. How do Proverbs 5:21 and 15:3 shed light on God's sovereignty? What does it mean to Christians that the Lord reigns over all? How does this affect the way we ought to live?

From the Commentary

> God's tender compassion and concern are seen in His care
> of the poor and needy. Widows and orphans in Israel were
> especially vulnerable to exploitation and abuse, and God
> warned His people in His law to beware of mistreating
> them (Ex. 22:22; Deut. 10:18; 14:29; 26:12; 27:19).
>
> "He who oppresses the poor reproaches his Maker, but he
> who honors Him has mercy on the needy" (Prov. 14:31
> NKJV; see 17:5). "The rich and the poor have this in com-
> mon, the LORD is the maker of them all" (22:2 NKJV).
> When the Savior came to earth, He identified with the
> poor and the outcasts (Luke 4:16–21; 2 Cor. 8:9), and
> God wants to show His compassion for them through
> His people. To harm the needy is to give pain to the heart
> of God.
>
> —*Be Skillful*, pages 195–96

7. Jesus talks about ministering to the poor throughout the Gospels. Why
is it significant that Solomon presents a similar message in Proverbs? What
do these messages, taken together, tell us about how we ought to respond
to poverty and to those who oppress the poor?

From the Commentary

One of God's compassionate ministries to us is that of *divine guidance*. Proverbs 3:5–6 is a promise God's people have been claiming for centuries, and it has never failed.... God expects us to assess a situation and get all the facts we can, but we must never lean on our own understanding. We must humble ourselves before Him and seek His direction in all things, and we must be sure that our motives are right.

But what if we make a mistake, as we're all prone to do, and start to move in the wrong direction? "In his heart a man plans his course, but the LORD determines his steps" (16:9 NIV). "Many are the plans in a man's heart, but it is the LORD's purpose that prevails" (19:21 NIV; see 16:33). If we sincerely want to know and obey God's plan, the Lord will direct us and providentially guide our steps in ways that we may not understand.

—*Be Skillful*, page 197

8. Read Proverbs 3:5–6. Is it easy to trust in the Lord with all your heart? Why or why not? What are the things in the heart that tend to make this difficult? What does it mean that God will make our paths straight? Does this mean we won't have trials or troubles? Explain.

From the Commentary

> God has revealed His wisdom in creation. "By wisdom
> the LORD laid the earth's foundations, by understanding
> he set the heavens in place; by his knowledge the deeps
> were divided, and the clouds let drop the dew" (Prov.
> 3:19–20 NIV). The astronomer watching a comet through
> a telescope and the biologist peering at a cell through a
> microscope are both discovering God's wisdom, for sci-
> entific study is but the act of thinking God's thoughts
> after Him.

—*Be Skillful*, page 198

9. Take a moment to consider the world around you, particularly nature
(3:19–20). What clues do you find in God's creation that reveal His
wisdom? List some examples. In what ways is science "the act of thinking
God's thoughts after Him"?

*More to Consider: Read Proverbs 21:30 and Job 12:13. What do these
verses tell us about God's providential ordering of events?*

From the Commentary

God wants to share His wisdom with us, which, of course, is the emphasis of the book of Proverbs. "For the LORD gives wisdom; from His mouth come knowledge and understanding; He stores up sound wisdom for the upright" (Prov. 2:6–7 NKJV). *The first step in receiving God's wisdom is trusting Jesus Christ and becoming a child of God.* The world is frantically seeking the wisdom to know what to do and the power to be able to do it, and these are found only in Jesus Christ, "the power of God, and the wisdom of God" (1 Cor. 1:24).

—*Be Skillful*, pages 199–200

10. In what ways do you see the world searching for wisdom? What sources do they mine to find that wisdom? If the first step to receiving God's wisdom is trusting Christ, what does that say about the role of the church today? How can your church help to open the minds and hearts of people in your community to the wisdom of God?

Looking Inward

Take a moment to reflect on all that you've explored thus far in this study of "Our God." Review your notes and answers and think about how each of these things matters in your life today.

Tips for Small Groups: To get the most out of this section, form pairs or trios and have group members take turns answering these questions. Be honest and as open as you can in this discussion, but most of all, be encouraging and supportive of others. Be sensitive to those who are going through particularly difficult times and don't press for people to speak if they're uncomfortable doing so.

11. Recall a time when you weren't trusting God. Where did you turn for wisdom to answer difficult questions? How is that different from the way you seek wisdom today? How does your relationship with Christ affect your ability to discover wisdom?

12. What is most difficult for you to understand about God's sovereignty? If God sees all and knows all, how does that affect the way you choose to live? In what ways is the truth of God's sovereignty comforting? In what ways might it be unsettling?

13. How are you living out God's command to take care of the poor? What are the practical things you're doing today to reach out to those in need? How is doing this an example of being wise? What are other ways you can take action on the God-written wisdom found in Proverbs and other books of the Bible?

Going Forward

14. Think of one or two things that you have learned that you'd like to work on in the coming week. Remember that this is all about quality, not quantity. It's better to work on one specific area of life and do it well than to work on many and do poorly (or to be so overwhelmed that you simply don't try).

Do you need to learn more about God's sovereignty? Do you need to put your wisdom into action? Be specific. Go back through the key verses in this lesson and put a star next to the phrase or verse that is most encouraging to you. Consider memorizing this verse.

Real-Life Application Ideas: Make a list of some of the most significant things you've learned throughout this study of Proverbs. Which of Solomon's wise sayings have helped you to feel confident in your faith? Which have challenged you? Make a list of these and then spend time with your list and in prayer every day for the coming week. Ask God to continually reveal His wisdom to you through Scripture.

Seeking Help

15. Write a prayer below (or simply pray one in silence), inviting God to work on your mind and heart in those areas you've previously noted. Be honest about your desires and fears.

Notes for Small Groups:
- *Look for ways to put into practice the things you wrote in the Going Forward section. Talk with other group members about your ideas and commit to being accountable to one another.*
- *During the coming week, ask the Holy Spirit to continue to reveal truth to you from what you've read and studied.*

Summary and Review

Notes for Small Groups: This session is a summary and review of this book. Because of that, it is shorter than the previous lessons. If you are using this in a small-group setting, consider combining this lesson with a time of fellowship or a shared meal.

Before you begin …
- *Pray for the Holy Spirit to reveal truth and wisdom as you go through this lesson.*
- *Briefly review the notes you made in the previous sessions. You will refer back to previous sections throughout this bonus lesson.*

Looking Back

1. Over the past ten lessons, you've examined the book of Proverbs. What expectations did you bring to this study? In what ways were those expectations met?

2. What is the most significant personal discovery you've made from this study?

3. What surprised you most about the pursuit of wisdom? What, if anything, troubled you?

Progress Report

4. Take a few moments to review the Going Forward sections of the previous lessons. How would you rate your progress for each of the things you chose to work on? What adjustments, if any, do you need to make to continue on the path toward spiritual maturity?

5. In what ways has your faith grown during this study? Take a moment to celebrate those things. Then think of areas where you feel you still need to grow and note those here. Make plans to revisit this study in a few weeks to review your growing faith.

Things to Pray About

6. Proverbs is about seeking and applying godly wisdom to your life. As you reflect on the words, ask God to reveal to you those truths that you most need to hear. Revisit the book often and seek the Holy Spirit's guidance to gain a better understanding of what it means to be wise.

7. The messages in Proverbs cover a wide variety of topics, including trusting God, avoiding popular sins, building healthy relationships, and more. Spend time praying about each of these topics.

8. Whether you've been studying this in a small group or on your own, there are many other Christians working through the very same issues you discovered when examining the book of Proverbs. Take time to pray for each of them, that God would reveal truth, that the Holy Spirit would guide you, and that each person might grow in spiritual maturity according to God's will.

A Blessing of Encouragement

Studying the Bible is one of the best ways to learn how to be more like Christ. Thanks for taking this step. In closing, let this blessing precede you and follow you into the next week while you continue to marinate in God's Word:

May God light your path to greater understanding as you review the truths found in the book of Proverbs and consider how they can help you grow closer to Christ.